ASPHYXIA
AND DROWNING
AN ATLAS

FORENSIC PATHOLOGY ATLASES
CAUSES OF DEATH SERIES

Series Editor: Jay Dix

Asphyxia and Drowning: An Atlas
Jay Dix, Michael Graham and Randy Hanzlick

Investigation of Road Traffic Fatalities: An Atlas
Jay Dix, Michael Graham and Randy Hanzlick

Time of Death, Decomposition and Identification: An Atlas
Jay Dix and Michael Graham

CAUSES OF DEATH ATLAS SERIES

ASPHYXIA AND DROWNING

AN ATLAS

JAY DIX,
MICHAEL GRAHAM
AND
RANDY HANZLICK

CRC Press
Taylor & Francis Group
Boca Raton   London   New York

CRC Press is an imprint of the
Taylor & Francis Group, an **informa** business

Library of Congress Cataloging-in-Publication Data

Catalog record is available from the Library of Congress.

Preface

Modern medicolegal death investigation involves a multidisciplinary team approach to gather pertinent historical and circumstantial information; recognize and document pertinent findings at the scene of injury/death; identify, recover and preserve potential evidentiary materials; and competently perform the appropriate examination of the victim, including laboratory and other special studies. The data are then correlated and interpreted in order to arrive at competent opinions as to the cause of death, manner of death and to address other pertinent issues. The various activities involved in death investigation are typically carried out by individuals with differing areas of expertise, training, education and experience — many with limited formal medical education. Preliminary information and observations in the early hours of a death investigation before the forensic pathologist reviews the case and examines the body may significantly help guide the death investigation to a successful conclusion if the pertinent data is sought, recognized and properly interpreted. On the other hand, mistakes in the early phases of a death investigation may significantly misdirect the procedure and may doom it to inadequacy or failure.

This atlas provides the reader with an overview of the types, mechanisms and physical findings associated with deaths involving asphyxia. The text serves as a basic framework upon which is built an extensive pictorial representation of findings associated with these types of deaths. It is written primarily for the lay death investigator and for law enforcement personnel involved in death investigation. It is also useful for pathologists (especially those without forensic training), interns and residents, attorneys and others with interest in this area.

The reader will gain a better understanding of the processes leading to asphyxiation, learn to recognize the physical findings associated with these conditions and better appreciate some of the difficulties in evaluating these deaths. Better understanding will lead to more efficient and effective investigations and foster improved communication between lay investigators and forensic pathologists.

M.G.

The Authors

Jay Dix, M.D. is Medical Examiner for Boone County, Missouri, and Associate Professor of Pathology/Chief of Forensic Pathology at the University of Missouri School of Medicine in Columbia. Dr. Dix has authored several outstanding books in the field of pathology and serves as a consultant to attorneys in both civil and criminal matters, and to coroners throughout Mid-Missouri.

Michael Graham, M.D. is the Chief Medical Examiner for the City of St. Louis, Missouri; Professor of Pathology at St. Louis University Health Sciences Center; and Co-Director of its Division of Forensic Pathology. He also serves as the Secretary-Treasurer of the National Association of Medical Examiners, and is a member of the Forensic Committee of the College of American Pathologists and a former officer of the Pathology/Biology Section of the American Academy of Forensic Sciences. Writer and editor of numerous scientific papers, book chapters and books, Dr. Graham is also on the Editorial Board of the *American Journal of Forensic Medicine and Pathology*. He is certified in anatomic, clinical and forensic pathology by the American Board of Pathology.

Randy Hanzlick, M.D. is Chief Medical Examiner for Fulton County, Georgia; Associate Professor of Forensic Pathology, Emory University School of Medicine, Atlanta; and Forensic Pathologist, Centers for Disease Control and Prevention, Atlanta. He has authored more than 150 scientific medical publications including articles, letters, chapters, books and manuals. His major areas of interest include forensic pathology and death investigation systems, training and guidelines. A board-certified forensic pathologist, Dr. Hanzlick is active in the National Association of Medical Examiners, the American Academy of Forensic Sciences and the College of American Pathologists.

Table of Contents

Asphyxia and Drowning

Introduction

Asphyxia is the loss of consciousness as the result of too little oxygen and, often, too much carbon dioxide in the blood. In current forensic medicine, asphyxia is the general term that encompasses a variety of conditions that have been traditionally thought of as having some defect in the uptake and/or utilization of oxygen.

To survive, a person must be able to take in oxygen, deliver it to the tissues, have the cells utilize the oxygen and eliminate unwanted byproducts. The process of moving air in and out of the lungs is called breathing. In order to breathe, there must be an open passage from the environment to the lungs, the chest must be able to expand to allow air movement into the lungs and the lungs must also be able to expand. Oxygen and carbon dioxide are transported to and from the tissues, including the lungs, through the circulation of blood. The cellular utilization of oxygen is involved in the metabolic processes of respiration. Defects leading to asphyxia can arise in any of these components.

Most types of asphyxia involve some defect in breathing, oxygen transport or respiration. However, asphyxia has been extended to include other entities, including some that primarily involve alteration in cerebral blood flow (e.g., neck compression), increased thoracic and cerebral vascular pressure (e.g., chest compression) and situations in which the environment lacks oxygen (vitiated atmosphere). Death due to asphyxia may be natural, homicidal, suicidal or accidental in nature.

Determination of the cause (and the manner) of deaths due to asphyxia requires, as in other types of deaths, correlating the physical findings, laboratory tests results, the information derived from the investigation of the scene of death and the pertinent circumstances surrounding the death, including the victim's past history, when pertinent. Asphyxial deaths are potentially associated with a large number of physical findings, reflecting the

1

broad scope of the causes of asphyxia. There are findings typical of asphyxia; however, these are nonspecific and can be found in other types of deaths. Some deaths due to asphyxia will have none of the characteristic findings.

The causes of asphyxia can be broadly categorized as mechanical or chemical. Mechanical asphyxia usually involves some physical force or abnormality affecting breathing or circulation. Chemical asphyxia usually involves a reaction between a chemical and the body, primarily resulting in interference with oxygen uptake, transport and/or utilization. In some types of asphyxia, deleterious effects may also be caused by the accompanying accumulation of carbon dioxide in the environment or in the blood.

There are numerous ways to further categorize the causes of asphyxia. In general, these classification systems have major categories that are based upon the nature of the predominant mechanism (e.g., airway obstruction, alteration in blood flow, etc.) and subcategories defined by other parameters such as the anatomic site of obstruction or nature of the applied force. Some types of asphyxia involve more than one mechanism. In addition, in any given case, more than one type of asphyxia may be present. The following classification is one the authors have found useful:

Mechanical Asphyxia

 I. Suffocation (cutting off the air supply)
  A. Vitiated atmosphere
  B. External airway
   1. Smothering
  C. Internal airway
   1. Choking
    a. Aspiration
   2. Airway swelling or obstruction
    a. Anaphylaxis
    b. Infection
    c. Mass (neoplastic and nonneoplastic)
    d. Chemical
    e. Trauma
    f. Mucus or debris
    g. Functional (bronchospasm)
   3. Airway compression
 II. Neck Compression (vascular and/or airway compression)
  A. Hanging
  B. Strangulation
   1. Manual (throttling)
   2. Ligature (garrotting)
   3. Yoking

  III. Chest Compression
        A. Compression (traumatic) asphyxia
  IV. Postural (positional)
   V. Miscellaneous

Chemical Asphyxia

   I. Oxygen uptake, delivery and transport
        A. Carbon monoxide
  II. Oxygen utilization
        A. Cyanide

Mechanical Asphyxia

Vitiated Atmosphere

A vitiated atmosphere, one in which adequate oxygen is lacking, may occur by displacement or depletion of oxygen. Oxygen can be displaced by other gases which may themselves be nontoxic, such as methane (natural gas), nitrogen or argon. The oxygen may also be consumed and reach insufficient atmospheric concentrations if it is not replenished. Consumption may be related to inanimate processes (e.g., rusting) or biologic ones (e.g., breathing and respiration). Carbon dioxide accumulation is often present when the oxygen has been depleted by human/animal consumption. Death can occur even though the victim's ability to breathe and respire are not impaired.

Displacement or depletion of atmospheric oxygen usually occurs in so-called closed spaces, such as wells, closed containers (e.g., refrigerators), large containers with poor air movement, improperly vented mine shafts or chemical storage tanks.

It is common to encounter multiple victims in these types of cases. Some of the victims may be intended rescuers who did not wear the appropriate safety equipment when attempting rescue and were also overcome by the lack of oxygen when they entered the oxygen-poor environment.

There are no physical signs to recognize a victim of a vitiated atmosphere. The postmortem measurement of the oxygen and/or carbon dioxide content of blood does not yield meaningful results. Routine drug screening does not include the measurement of biologically inert gases such as those noted above. In some cases, the displacing gas may be found in samples of air obtained from the lungs or, rarely, from the victim's blood. Reliable postmortem air sampling is often compromised by the efforts of rescue and medical personnel to revive the victim.

The diagnosis of death related to a vitiated atmosphere is predominately made by the history and scene investigation. In some cases, it may be possible to measure the oxygen content of the atmosphere. However, in most cases this is not possible due to the introduction of oxygen during rescue efforts.

Smothering

Smothering is the obstruction to the passage of air by occlusion of the mouth and/or nose. Some pathologists also include instances involving occlusion of the oropharynx (upper throat area where the nose and mouth cavities merge) as smothering. The occlusion can be caused by many different types of objects, including such things as the hand, a pillow, a plastic bag or dirt (e.g., ditch cave-in). Occasionally, material from the suffocating object may be found in or around the nose/mouth. In addition, some cases of smothering involve occlusion of the upper throat by the tongue, such as may occur when a gag is forcibly placed in the mouth or the lower jaw of an infant is pushed backward.

The extent of injury in smothering is variable. In some cases, there may be minimal or no external injuries. When injuries are present, those directly related to the obstruction are typically found in the central facial area and include such things as abrasions/contusions of the nose, cheeks, chin, inner surface of the mouth and inner surface of the cheeks. In addition, there may also be injuries incurred by the victim struggling to prevent being smothered. Injuries related to smothering often reflect the inexperience of the assailant (i.e., the use of more force than is necessary) and the extent of struggle by the victim. Pinpoint hemorrhages (petechiae) may occasionally be found on the face (especially the eyelid area), gingiva and eyes — but may just as easily be absent.

Smothering may be homicidal, accidental or suicidal. Smothering is a common form of asphyxical homicide among children. Investigation plays an important role in determining the manner of death in these cases since each manner of death may have the same physical findings. For example, a plastic bag encasing the head of a young adult may represent homicide if the bag was purposefully placed there by someone else; an accident if the bag was being used for recreational sexual stimulation; or a suicide if the victim placed the bag in order to take his or her own life. Covering the head with a plastic bag may involve more than one type of asphyxia. There may be occlusion of airflow (smothering) and/or depletion of oxygen (vitiated atmosphere).

Choking

Choking involves blockage of the internal airway — posterior pharynx, larynx (voicebox), trachea (windpipe), bronchi — by a foreign material.

If the foreign material is an object, in adults it is generally not inhaled but, instead, is impacted deep in the throat (posterior pharynx) where it occludes the opening straddling the larynx and the esophagus. The individual may be able to exhale but cannot inhale since the object functions as a ball valve. For this reason, forcibly expelling air from the lungs or stomach may dislodge the object and prevent death (e.g., Heimlich maneuver). In contrast, choking in children often involves the inhalation (aspiration) of a small object into the airway.

Adults who choke on an object or bolus are usually impaired by such conditions as intoxication (ethanol or other depressant), neurologic disease, senility, mental illness or dentures. The impairment usually involves swallowing or protecting the airway; it may also involve forces that overwhelm the swallowing/airway protection mechanism, such as may occur with self-induced forced feeding in a psychotic patient. A classic example of choking is the "café coronary," which is usually caused by a large piece of inadequately chewed meat lodging in the throat of a diner who is drunk. In contrast, children who lethally choke are typically not impaired. Children are most at risk for choking because they have small-diameter airways and have a propensity to put small objects within and around the mouth area.

Aspiration of less discrete materials can also occur. Perhaps the most common of these is the aspiration of gastric contents, which although frequently seen is still a very unusual cause of an asphyxial death. Unimpaired adults and children do not lethally aspirate their gastric contents. Aspiration of gastric contents most commonly occurs as an agonal or postmortem event in individuals dying of unrelated conditions. Agonal gastric aspiration may hinder resuscitation efforts and may cause severe respiratory problems in surviving persons. However, aspiration of gastric contents may occur as an antemortem clinically significant event. When it does, it is usually in the setting of impaired consciousness with inadequate airway protection such as may be seen in patients with head injuries, under the influence of ethanol/drugs or undergoing general anesthesia.

Not all aspirated material is foreign to the body, although it may be foreign to the airway. Aspiration of blood from the injuries to the head or neck may result in blockage of the airway.

Most deaths due to choking are accidental. However, occasionally choking may be homicidal. Examples of homicidal choking include force-feeding and occlusion of the airway by a gag. Some gags, such as washcloths, may permit the passage of air when they are dry but become less permeable and occlusive as they become saturated with saliva. Aspiration of punitively administered pepper has caused the death of several children. In the case of pepper aspiration, airway obstruction is caused not only by the mass of the pepper impacted in the airway but also by airway swelling caused by the irritant properties of the pepper.

Airway Swelling and Obstruction

Obstruction to the passage of air may occur when there is sufficient swelling of tissues around or lining the airway. Swelling of the narrowest parts of the airway is usually involved in these cases. Typically, the swelling will involve the larynx, the soft tissues immediately above the larynx or the smaller air passages within the lungs (bronchi and/or bronchioles). Airway swelling may be caused by a number of conditions.

An acute allergic reaction of a particular type called anaphylaxis may result in prominent swelling of the larynx and the soft tissues around the opening to the larynx. The swelling may be extensive enough to sufficiently impede the passage of air through the larynx and cause death. Examples of allergic reactions involving anaphylaxis include those following the administration of penicillin to susceptible individuals or following a bee sting to someone allergic to bee venom.

Infections may also result in lethal swelling of the airway. Bacterial infection (acute epiglottitis) of the structure guarding the opening to the airway (epiglottis) causes inflammatory swelling that may occlude the airway. Viral infections to the small airways (small bronchi and bronchioles), especially in children, may also result in significant airway obstruction. Obstruction complicating small airway infections is often the result of a combination of airway swelling, obstruction by mucus and inflammatory debris and narrowing by spasm of the muscle within the wall of the airway.

A mass, such as a tumor, may grow within the airway and block the passage of air, leading to asphyxia. Tumors leading to asphyxia in this way are usually found in the larynx or trachea.

Irritating substances such as pepper or other chemical agents introduced into the airway may cause the inner lining of the airway to swell and impede the passage of air. Obstruction may be further complicated by mucus, inflammatory debris and spasm. Obstruction occurring in this manner is usually at the level of the larynx and/or small airways.

The airway, usually at the larynx, may swell as a result of direct injury such as a blow to the neck. In these cases, there is usually a delay of minutes or hours between the injury and the onset of asphyxia.

Obstructing the small airways may also lead to asphxyia. Small airway obstruction can be mechanical, functional or, commonly, a combination of both. As noted above, the small airways may be occluded by the presence of inflammatory debris or mucus. In asthma, the small airways are typically occluded by plugs of mucus as well as by narrowing due to contraction of the airway muscle fibers (bronchoconstriction or bronchospasm).

Asphyxia may also occur if a mass extrinsic to the airway exerts pressure on it and compresses it. Masses extrinsic to the airway include such things as hematomas and tumors.

Neck Compression

Hanging and strangulation cause asphyxia by compressing vital structures within the neck. Although the airway may be compressed in deaths due to hanging or strangulation, it is compression of the major blood vessels within the neck (jugular veins and carotid arteries) that appears to be most responsible for the onset of unconsciousness and death. It takes about 4.4 pounds of properly applied pressure to occlude the jugular veins, 7 pounds to occlude the carotid arteries and 33 pounds to occlude the adult trachea. The airway of a child is more compressible than that of an adult. Airway compression is not necessary for either unconsciousness or death to occur. There are a number of deaths related to hanging that have occurred in people with tracheostomies in which the ligatures were located above the tracheostomy sites — thus, these people died strictly due to compression of the neck blood vessels since the tracheostomy allowed them to breathe even after the ligature was in place.

Hanging

During hanging, the force on the neck is caused by the weight of the victim's body. The force is transmitted through some sort of ligature such as a noose, portions of a defective crib or a branch point/crotch of a tree. There are two forms of hanging — judicial and nonjudicial.

Judicial hanging involves a drop with a sudden stop at the end of the rope. The judicial hanging system is designed to cause a fracture-dislocation of the upper cervical spine with lethal damage to the upper cervical spinal cord and/or brainstem. Properly carried out, unconsciousness, if not death, is instantaneous. Judicial hangings will not be discussed further in this atlas. Henceforth, the term "hanging" will refer to nonjudicial hanging.

In contrast, nonjudicial hangings that are extremely common do not entail a drop or a broken neck but cause death by compression of the major blood vessels (with or without airway compromise) of the neck. Since it takes relatively little pressure to cause death in this way, complete suspension of the body is not necessary. In fact, many people who die from hanging are not fully suspended. Their feet, if not their legs and buttocks, are usually in contact with the ground or floor. Unconsciousness occurs very rapidly when the carotid arteries are occluded. Unconsciousness may be delayed for a short period of time if only the jugular veins are compressed or in the event that only the airway is compressed (e.g., ligature device design that results in airway compression while protecting the integrity of the blood vessels).

The most common external injury in a hanging is a ligature mark. The appearance of the mark is quite variable. It can range in appearance from a slight depression on the neck to a prominently abraded deep furrow. The appearance of the ligature mark will depend on many factors, including the width of the ligature, its "softness," its smoothness, the amount of force exerted on the neck, the length of time the body remains suspended, whether or not a drop from some height was involved and whether any material, such as clothing, was interposed between the ligature and the skin. In general, bodies that have been fully suspended for many hours by a thin firm ligature will leave the most prominent marks. A broad soft ligature, such as a soft towel, may cause minimal marking or leave no mark at all.

Many ligature marks will bear the pattern of the ligature — the weave of a cloth rope, configuration of electrical wiring or the design on a belt. The mark may be red or yellow-tan. The yellow-tan appearance may suggest the mark was made postmortem and that the person was killed in some way and then the body was hanged. In fact, many ligature marks are predominately made after death as the person who died by hanging within minutes of initial suspension remains suspended until the body is found and released. During this time, which is often several hours, the ligature continues to apply pressure to the skin, resulting in the creation of a prominent postmortem ligature mark. The arms of the ligature mark in hanging are usually diagonally oriented around the neck (since most people hang with the upper body in the vertical position), encircle the neck except under the point of suspension where the ligature is often pulled away from the skin surface and are usually located at or above the level of the thyroid cartilage (Adam's apple). The arms of the mark passing around the neck climb toward the point of suspension. Occasionally, the mark around the neck may be horizontal in hanging — for example, when a person ties the rope to the bed canopy, lies in bed and hangs his or her head over the end of the bed. Since horizontal marks around the neck suggest ligature strangulation, it is important for the pathologist to know how the body was suspended so the mark around the neck, especially if it is in an atypical position or configuration, can be appropriately interpreted. There may be some bruising along a ligature mark; however, prominent bruising of the skin, especially away from the ligature mark, is not a feature of hanging. The knot may also leave a mark on the neck. Ligatures in place around the neck should be removed in such a way so as not to disrupt the knot. This helps to facilitate reconstruction of the event and to determine if the victim could potentially tie the knot and secure the noose.

The face and neck above the level of the ligature may be congested and appear dusky purple if the jugular veins were compressed for a period of time before the carotid arteries were compressed, thus allowing blood to flow into the head but restricting its exit from the head. In these cases, some petechiae may be found on the face (usually around the orbits), conjunctivae and, occasionally, the gingiva. However, in most instances of hanging, the jugular veins and carotid arteries appear to become compressed at essentially the same time; thus, in most hanging deaths the face is relatively pale (except for the usual livor mortis) and petechiae are absent above the level of the ligature.

Livor mortis in someone who has been suspended for hours should be most prominent in the lower half of the body, notably in the distal portions of the extremities. As the blood vessels distend with blood during the formation and intensification of livor, some of the blood vessels will break, causing small areas of apparent bleeding in the skin. These postmortem areas of extravasation (pseudohemorrhage) are known as Tardieu spots.

Victims of hanging often have protrusion of the tongue. The protruding segment of the tongue is often red, red-black or black. The protrusion is due to the noose pushing the larynx upward as the body sags under the influence of gravity. The relative upward movement of the larynx forces the tongue, to which it is ultimately connected, out of the mouth. The discoloration of the protruding segment of the tongue is due to atmospheric drying of the normally moist tongue surface.

Injuries to the internal neck structures in nonjudicial hangings are typically minimal or absent, reflecting the relatively gentle sustained localized nature of the pressure involved in hanging. Minimal hemorrhage within the soft tissues of the neck is occasionally found; however, in most cases, there is no hemorrhage in the soft tissues of the neck. An exception to this is occasionally seen in hanging, involving a drop prior to suspension such as may occur if someone jumps from the balcony with a noose around the neck — essentially, this turns a nonjudicial hanging into a quasi-judicial hanging. The larynx and hyoid bone are typically intact in hangings, as is the cervical spine. Rarely, these other neck structures may be damaged in a hanging involving a drop, especially if the victim is elderly and these structures are more brittle.

The vast majority of nonjudicial hangings are suicides. Homicide by hanging is rare. An occasional hanging death is accidental. These accidental hangings may occur in infants (often related to a broken/defective crib or suspension by a pacifier cord), youngsters "fooling around" or adults (sometimes children) during autoerotic activity.

Autoeroticism involves solo sexual activity in which some device is used to enhance sexual stimulation. Some individuals claim that sexual arousal is enhanced when the brain is getting less than the ideal amount of oxygen (hypoxia). Thus, autoeroticism traditionally involves the use of some controllable method for inducing nonlethal asphyxia. Death occurs when consciousness is inadvertently lost or the escape mechanism fails, leading to lethal asphyxia. Hanging is the most common cause of death during autoerotic activity. Often, the skin will be protected from the ligature by the use of padding, such as a towel. However, the presence of padding does not necessarily indicate death was accidental since an occasional suicide victim will pad the noose to reduce discomfort while dying. Occasional deaths due to suffocation occur. Not all the enhancing devices or deaths are asphyxial in nature. Deaths related to the use of electrical devices have also occurred during autoerotic activity. Autoerotic deaths typically involve young adult males; however, we have examined autoerotic deaths involving children and the elderly. Autoerotic deaths among females are rare.

The scene investigation often reveals pornography, some degree of nudity which may be as little as genital exposure, cross-dressing, bondage and/or the use of other props or paraphernalia. These scenes and the "equipment" used may be complex and bizarre. There is often indication that this type of behavior has occurred many times in the past. The complexity of the scenario may indicate repetition and "maturing" of the activity, or repetitive activity may be physically demonstrated by finding grooves worn in the rafters where suspension had occurred in the past. Whatever the device in use happens to be or whatever activity is being carried out, there is some sort of escape to prevent lethal asphyxia. The escape may involve nothing more than removing a plastic bag from the head or standing up to relieve pressure on the neck. In other cases, the escape mechanism may be relatively complex. Individuals who die during this type of activity are attempting only to have a satisfying sexual experience and are not intending to die — thus, their deaths are properly certified as accidents.

Strangulation

In strangulation, some outside force (not the weight of the victim's body) places pressure on the neck. Strangulation is often categorized as manual, ligature or yoking. In some cases, more than one type of strangulation may have occurred. Unconsciousness and death may be due to compression of the blood vessels in the neck and/or compression of the airway. The rapidity of the onset of unconsciousness will depend on how extensively, how effectively, how rapidly and which structures in the neck are compressed. Rapid effective compression of the carotid arteries will result in the rapid onset of unconsciousness. The pressure on the neck must be maintained for some period of time for death to occur. The time it takes for death to occur is variable and can only be estimated in a general sense by the forensic pathologist, who should not render an opinion as to the exact length of time until unconsciousness or death. In rare cases, pressure exerted on the neck may stimulate the carotid sinus, resulting in increased vagus nerve activity which can slow the heart rate. In general, continued pressure on the carotid sinus does not result in stoppage of a normal heart. There are rare individuals who have reasonably well-documented episodes of cardiac arrest that appear to have been precipitated by stimulation of an abnormally sensitive carotid sinus. These individuals have structurally normal hearts and almost invariably have a prior history of episodic dizziness or passing out (syncope) related to pressure, often mild, on the neck. In contrast, stimulation of the carotid sinus of a person having heart disease may precipitate, albeit rarely, a lethal cardiac rhythm disturbance.

Manual Strangulation

Manual strangulation (throttling) involves the use of the hands to compress the neck. In most, but not all, deaths due to manual strangulation there will be injury to the external and usually the internal structures of the neck. A variety of marks may be seen on the skin of the neck, including nonspecific abrasions, nonspecific contusions, round-oval contusions suggestive of fingerpad marks and fingernail marks. It should be remembered that fingernail marks on the neck are not necessarily those of the assailant. The victim may leave fingernail marks on his or her own neck, for example, while trying to relieve pressure being applied by the assailant. It is not possible to tell if the assailant is right or left handed or the absolute positions of the victim and assailant, since most adults are capable of applying sufficient pressure to the neck to cause death with either hand, on the forehand or the backhand and from the front, back or side. Marks on the mouth and other areas of the face are also common in deaths involving manual strangulation. Petechiae are typically present on the face, conjunctivae and/or gingiva.

The internal neck structures may also be damaged. The internal neck structures are most effectively examined through a layer-by-layer dissection that is performed after the chest and cranial contents have been removed. This technique allows the blood to drain from the neck's blood vessels and minimizes or eliminates artifactual hemorrhages caused by the dissection. Hemorrhage is often, but not invariably, present within the soft tissues of the neck. The hemorrhage is often rather extensive, reflecting the application of a large amount of force and movement between the victim and the assailant, leading to inefficiency in maintaining a constant steady grip/pressure. Mild or absent soft tissue hemorrhage suggests a disparity between the assailant and the victim, such as may be seen in an adult man strangling a baby, an elderly debilitated person or an intoxicated adult. Damage to other internal neck structures is also common. There are often fractures of the larynx and/or hyoid bone. The probability of fracturing these structures is related to their rigidity and brittleness. In infants and children, these structures are predominately cartilagenous and are, thus, very flexible and difficult to break. As a person passes through adulthood, these structures become more bony and are thus more rigid and brittle, increasing their susceptibility to fracture. Thus, fractures of these structures are rare in children, become more common in young adults and are very common in the elderly. Hemorrhage within the tongue is also common in manual strangulation.

Ligature Strangulation

Ligature strangulation (garotting) may cause findings seen in hanging and manual strangulation. A ligature mark is often, but not always, present. The appearance of a ligature mark will reflect the nature of the ligature (soft or firm, narrow or broad, smooth or rough, surface pattern) and the force applied to the neck. For example, a narrow ligature will tend to create a distinct narrow mark. Sometimes, material from the ligature will be embedded in the skin. In contrast to the typical mark in hanging, the ligature mark in garotting tends to be lower on the neck and oriented horizontally. The typical ligature mark is relatively well localized since it is usually relatively easy to keep the ligature in one place on the neck during the strangulation. If the ligature does not efficiently "grip" the neck there may be multiple ligature marks or atypical marks. If the ligature is in place, it should be removed in such a way so as not to disrupt the knot. The structure of the knot, especially if an unusual or complex one, may help link a particular ligature strangulation to others perpetrated by the same assailant. Petechiae are often present on the face, conjunctivae and gingiva and the face may appear somewhat congested. However, if the carotid arteries are effectively rapidly compressed, petechiae and plethora may be absent.

The internal structures of the neck are also likely to display evidence of injury, although this is not invariably the case. Although uncommon, it is possible to garotte someone without leaving marks on the outside or the inside of the neck. Soft tissue hemorrhage within the neck is variable and ranges from absent to severe. Overall, it is somewhat less prominent than in manual strangulation. Fractures of the larynx occasionally occur during ligature strangulation. Hyoid bone fractures are unusual.

Yoking

Yoking is the compression of the anterior neck using the forearm, often from behind. Traditional restraint holds (crossbar or choke hold, lateral neck restraint or carotid sleeper hold) are types of yoking. Properly and efficiently applied, the lateral neck restraint hold induces unconsciousness within 15 seconds by compressing the carotid arteries. As with other forms of neck compression, the onset of unconsciousness depends on what structures are compressed and how effectively and efficiently the compression takes place.

Injury to the skin of the neck may be absent in yoking since the pressure is being applied by a broad soft object, the forearm. However, bruising may occur, especially if there is movement between the victim and assailant and a large amount of force is applied. Similarly, damage to internal neck structures is also quite variable. Petechiae are often present but are not invariable.

Occasionally, fatal neck compression is caused by forcing an object such as a board or rigid bar against the front of the neck. These deaths often are associated with prominent injury to the external and internal aspects of the neck.

The manner of death in the vast majority of lethal strangulations is homicide. Occasionally, a child may accidentally strangle when something around the neck becomes entangled or an adult may be involved in an industrial accident in which a cable encircles and compresses the neck. In some sex-related deaths, the lethal event may involve neck compression, postural mechanisms or other mechanisms. Some of these deaths may also involve chemical asphyxia (e.g., nitrous oxide inhalation) and other substance abuse, often alcohol and cocaine. In such cases, the intent of the offender is not always clear because there may have been some degree of consent on the part of the victim to risky behavior. Suicidal asphyxiation by manual strangulation is not possible. Once hypoxia sufficient to cause unconsciousness occurs, but not sufficient to cause prolonged unconsciousness or death, the pressure on the neck will be relieved. Ligature strangulation can be employed as a means of suicide if the ligature is secured around the neck in such a way as to maintain pressure after consciousness is lost.

Chest Compression

Compression of the chest or upper abdomen can cause death by hindering breathing or increasing intrathoracic pressure. This type of asphyxia is sometimes referred to as "traumatic" asphyxia. We prefer not to use the term "traumatic" asphyxia since many of the other types of asphyxia are certainly traumatic in nature. We prefer the term "compression asphyxia" since it more accurately describes the nature of the asphyxic event. The mechanism of death and the physical findings will be determined, in part, by the amount of exerted pressure.

When extreme pressure is suddenly exerted on the chest, such as when a car slips off the jack and comes to rest on the mechanic's chest, there is a sudden increase in pressure inside the chest. Markedly increased intrathoracic pressure may detrimentally affect cardiac hemodynamics, especially of the normally low pressure right side of the heart. Pressure is also transmitted backward through the veins. The result of this increase in venous pressure leads to the characteristic physical findings of marked dusky congestion of the head and neck and petechiae which are most numerous on the face and conjunctivae. It is not uncommon to also see petechiae on the shoulders and upper chest. The rapid increase in venous pressure is also transmitted to the brain and may result in the rapid, even immediate, onset of unconsciousness. The very rapid onset of unconsciousness is due to the effects of the increased pressure on the brain and is not primarily due to asphyxia. If the pressure on the chest is maintained, asphyxia can occur due to the hindering of breathing by the victim's inability to expand the chest. In addition to the findings noted above, there are often small hemorrhages in the muscles of the neck and chest near points of attachment to bone. Marks also may be made on the torso by the compressing agent. Injuries to ribs and internal organs are variable. In some cases, there may be fractured ribs and/or lacerated organs; however, in other cases, no internal injuries are present.

When less pressure is applied to the chest or upper abdomen such that the chest is unable to expand during inspiration but intrathoracic pressures are not significantly increased, death is caused by the inability to breathe. In these cases, physical findings may be lacking and the determination of the cause of death rests heavily on the investigation of the scene and circumstances of death. Thus, infants dying because of overlying may exhibit no external signs of injury. In many cases, however, the victim will forcefully attempt to maintain breathing and, in doing so, will increase pressure within the chest leading to congestion and petechiae, typically most evident on the face and conjunctivae. Internal injuries are typically lacking in these deaths.

Compression of the chest with intermediate degrees of pressure is common and leads to inhibition of breathing and less extreme increases in intrathoracic pressure. A classic example of this type of pressure is that exerted by a constricting snake, such as a python. The snake coils around the body and exerts enough pressure to inhibit chest expansion during inspiration. As the victim exhales and the chest becomes smaller, the snake tightens to further hinder inspiration by restricting the ability of the chest to expand. In these cases, congestion and petechiae are usually prominent. Internal injuries are usually lacking or, if present, are minor in these cases.

Postural (Positional) Asphyxia

Postural asphyxia occurs when the position of the body is such that adequate breathing cannot be maintained. This most commonly occurs when the head is markedly flexed to the extent that the chin touches the upper chest. The airway may be blocked in this position. In addition, in some of these cases there may also be some element of vascular compromise. Asphyxia can also result from a person being in the head-down vertical position for an extended period of time. In this position, fatigue of the muscles needed to breathe develops along with hemodynamic compromise. Examples of this type of postural asphyxia include a driver in a motor vehicle crash trapped sitting behind the wheel in an upside-down car or someone crucified in the upside-down position. Rarely, postural asphyxia occurs in the upright position due to unremitting fatigue of the breathing musculature as may occur in upright crucifixion. Accidental postural asphyxia exclusive of that occurring in vehicles is commonly associated with ethanol intoxication.

Miscellaneous

Asphyxia can be an effect of other injuries causing ineffective breathing, such as a flail chest or ruptured diaphragm. These deaths are usually classified as being due to the particular injury (e.g., thoracic blunt trauma) and are not usually considered primary asphyxial deaths, notwithstanding that the actual mechanism of death may involve asphyxia. Some pathologists refer to this type of asphyxia as "traumatic asphyxia."

Asphyxia can also result from a variety of disease processes affecting the lungs that physically inhibit the transfer of oxygen from the inspired air into the blood, such as may occur when scar tissue forms within the walls of many of the airsacs. Examples of these diseases include idiopathic diffuse interstitial pulmonary fibrosis and radiation-induced pulmonary fibrosis. Emphysema can also cause asphyxia by destroying lung tissue and altering the normal matched distribution of blood to air.

Chemical Asphyxia

As previously noted, chemical asphyxia involves a reaction between a chemical and the body, resulting primarily in interference with oxygen uptake, transport and/or utilization. The buildup and failure to eliminate toxic products of metabolism is also commonly present and may also be damaging to the body. The chemical agent may act locally to damage the lung tissue where gas exchange occurs and/or it may act systemically to affect oxygen transport, cellular uptake and/or utilization. Systemic chemical asphyxia predominately targets respiration, although there may be secondary effects on breathing.

Carbon Monoxide

Carbon monoxide (CO) is an odorless, colorless and tasteless gas that is a byproduct of the incomplete combustion of materials containing carbon. It binds to hemoglobin, the substance in the blood responsible for carrying oxygen, with an affinity approximately 240 times that of oxygen, thus inhibiting the uptake and transport of oxygen by the blood. Carbon monoxide also binds more avidly with myoglobin (an oxygen binding structure in muscle tissue) than does oxygen. Carbon monoxide also inhibits the transfer of oxygen into the cells of the body by making it more difficult for hemoglobin to release whatever oxygen is bound to it. Lastly, carbon monoxide interferes with some of the respiratory processes within the cells.

The most common cause of death involving carbon monoxide toxicity is smoke inhalation during a structural fire. Carbon monoxide is the major toxicant in this type of fire, but it is not the only dangerous substance in smoke. Most victims of house fires die or are unconscious from smoke inhalation prior to sustaining burns. Suicide by inhaling motor vehicle exhaust is another common scenario involving carbon monoxide toxicity. Accidental carbon monoxide toxicity may be seen in situations such as a malfunctioning furnace or heater, a demented person forgetting to turn off the car after parking it in an attached garage and, rarely, as a complication of open air fires.

Carbon monoxide is not produced or absorbed to any significant degree after death, regardless of the atmospheric concentration. Thus, postmortem carbon monoxide test results accurately reflect the amount of hemoglobin saturated with carbon monoxide at the time of death. A normal person has less than 5% of his or her hemoglobin saturated by CO (COHb). A person who smokes may have up to 10% saturation, although some heavy smokers may reach 15% hemoglobin saturation. It has been noted that there is poor correlation between COHb levels and clinical symptoms. However, in general, lethality occurs in healthy middle-aged adults when COHb levels exceed 50 to 60%. It is not unusual to find COHb levels of 70 to 80% in individuals dying of carbon monoxide inhalation. Death may occur at much lower concentrations if the victim has pre-existing diseases, such as heart or lung disease, or if they are impaired by ethanol or other depressant-type toxicants or some other toxic agents. COHb test results must be interpreted with caution in individuals who have survived for some period of time following their removal from the carbon monoxide source, especially if they received medical care involving the administration of oxygen. The normal half-life of CO is 5 to 6 hours. However, with certain types of oxygen therapy this may be reduced to approximately 40 minutes.

The livor mortis of people dying of carbon monoxide poisoning is characteristically cherry red or red-pink. This color is usually visible when the COHb is at least 30%. In bodies covered with soot or having darkly pigmented skin, the red-pink color may be evident in the nailbeds and in the lining of the mouth. During the examination of the internal portions of the body the muscles and blood tend to be lighter red than usual. The presence of bright red livor does not necessarily indicate that CO-similar coloration may be present in other conditions such as cyanide poisoning and bodies that have been in refrigerated storage.

Many victims of lethal carbon monoxide poisoning will have areas in which the outer layers of the skin have separated from the deeper layers. The outer layers then slip off or are easily dislodged during manipulation of the body, resulting in exposure of the deeper layers. The exposed deep layers may be red or gray-tan. This epidermal slippage phenomenon typically is a postmortem event. Occasionally, blister formation occurs in a living individual who is in a CO or drug-induced coma. Areas of postmortem epidermal slippage are commonly misinterpreted as antemortem partial thickness thermal burns. The phenomenon of epidermal slippage is not specific for CO poisoning.

Cyanide

Cyanide disrupts the ability of cells to utilize oxygen by binding to and inhibiting the cellular respiratory enzyme mitochondrial cytochrome oxidase. Cyanide poisoning most rapidly and severely affects the brain and the heart. In fatalities, the onset of symptoms and progression to death is usually rapid, especially if the cyanide is inhaled. Consciousness may be suddenly lost after only a few breaths containing a high concentration of cyanide. The onset of symptoms may be delayed if the cyanide is ingested.

The body of someone who has died of cyanide poisoning may appear a "healthy" pink or cherry red, much like that associated with carbon monoxide poisoning. However, in contrast to carbon monoxide poisoning, the pink color in cyanide poisoning is due to the presence of fully oxygenated blood since cyanide inhibits the extraction of oxygen from the blood by the tissues. The presence of cyanosis, however, does not exclude cyanide poisoning since victims of cyanide poisoning may develop cyanosis.

Some cyanide victims may be recognized as having an aroma often described as "bitter almonds" or "musty." Not all people are capable of smelling this aroma.

Some cyanide compounds are corrosive. An individual ingesting one of these compounds may have corrosive injuries involving the oral cavity and/or hemorrhage of the inner lining (mucosa) of the stomach.

Drowning

Drowning is death due to submersion in a liquid, usually water. The submersion does not have to be total. Drowning can also occur when only part of the body is in the liquid as may occur, for example, to a person face-down in shallow water. Although drowning is a form of asphyxia, the mechanisms involved in drowning may include factors other than asphyxia and the physical findings at autopsy differ somewhat from those in other typical forms of asphyxia.

Drowning is characterized initially, especially in cold water, by a period of panic and hyperventilation. Breath-holding may be attempted but at some point, depending on blood oxygen and carbon dioxide concentrations, involuntary respirations will occur. Uncontrollable hyperventilation may lead to aspiration of large quantities of water and may hasten hypothermia if the aspirated water is cold. A large volume of water may also be swallowed, which increases the risk of vomiting and aspiration of gastric contents. Most people who are drowning will exhibit violent struggling prior to losing consciousness. Once unconsciousness occurs, water can passively enter the airway.

The hypoxia that occurs during drowning is caused by water aspiration or laryngospasm. Water aspiration is responsible for the hypoxia in approximately 85 to 90% of drownings (so-called "wet lung" drownings) whereas laryngospasm causes the hypoxia in the other 10 to 15% (so-called "dry lung" drownings).

The aspiration of water causes numerous alterations in the lung that lead to hypoxia. These include the presence of liquid within the airspaces and interstitium, the loss of surfactant (a chemical lining the lungs that is involved in maintaining surface tension and airspace expansion), the presence of protein-rich material in the airways and airspaces and damage to the air-blood interface. Damage may also be done by inhaled contaminants, chemicals and bacteria. Some of the damage may not become apparent unless the patient survives for several hours or days.

Rarely, sudden death may occur when someone jumps or dives into cold water. In these cases, activation of cold receptors in the skin leads to cardiac arrest mediated by the vagus nerve.

Drowning can occur in any type of water — fresh, salt or brackish. When fresh water is aspirated, the water rapidly moves from the airspaces into the blood vessels, removes surfactant and damages the cells lining the air sacs. In contrast, when salt water is inhaled, fluid moves from the blood vessels into the lung tissue and air spaces, leading to the rapid onset of pulmonary edema. Although movement of water into or out of the circulation conceivably could alter the blood's salt concentrations, this does not seem to be a major problem from a clinical standpoint in the vast majority of drowning episodes. However, the role, if any, of these electrolyte changes in persons dead in the water is not known. In general, it appears that the amount of water aspirated is more significant than the type of water.

A number of questions arise from deaths occurring in the water — how and why did the person get into the water, what happened while in the water and why didn't the person get out of the water? An additional question may arise in some deaths — was the person alive when entering the water?

Although considerable variations exist, most drowning victims and drowning episodes fit within a limited number of well-recognized scenarios. Most drowning victims are male and are most likely to be either toddlers or teenagers. Healthy adults who can swim rarely drown unless there is an intervening reason to make them less likely to survive in the water, such as natural disease, alcohol/drugs, injury or engaging in activity beyond their capabilities or in a dangerous environment. The vast majority of drownings are accidental, while about 10% are suicidal and less than 1% are homicidal.

The investigation of the circumstances and the scene of death are paramount in properly establishing not only the cause of death but also the manner of death since the autopsy findings of a drowning victim may well be identical if the victim jumped, fell or was pushed into the water. Since man by nature is not an aquatic animal, human excursions into water may be viewed as man vs. a hostile environment. Investigating death by drowning involves determining what human and environmental factors prevented the victim from leaving the water alive and healthy.

Human factors that need to be assessed include such things as the victim's age, level of fitness, history of previous behavior (e.g., risk-taking, etc.), pre-swim activities (e.g., hyperventilation), swimming ability and experience, potentially debilitating or incapacitating diseases (physical and/or mental) or injuries that may either lead to drowning or hinder survival efforts (e.g., asthma, seizure disorder, neck injury), the presence of toxicants (most commonly ethanol) that may lead to careless behavior or ineffective survival efforts, clothing and equipment status. Environmental factors to consider include such things as water temperature, current, terrain, water depth, floating objects (including boats) and the presence of injurious animals or plants. Additional factors come into play in deaths during scuba diving. A discussion of the investigation of scuba deaths is beyond the scope of this atlas.

In addition to the investigative information about the victim and the scene as described above, witnesses' accounts may also be helpful. For example, sudden collapse or sinking in the water without any struggle or evident survival efforts suggests sudden death or incapacitation unrelated to the water. Similar inactivity after diving into shallow water may point to the presence of an incapacitating or lethal head or neck injury. Similarly, sudden collapse of a scuba diver immediately upon surfacing suggests air embolism.

The appropriateness of the victim to the location may also offer insight into the nature of the death — thus, a farmer with severe heart disease found floating in the water adjacent to the bank next to his fishing pole in a secluded pond would be far less suspicious than a man wearing a tuxedo floating in the same pond.

Most of the findings at autopsy are due to the body being in water, regardless of whether or not death was caused by drowning. In addition, the typical postmortem changes that occur may be altered due to water immersion.

The hair and clothing are usually wet unless the body has washed up or has otherwise been removed from the water or the water has receded (e.g., flooded stream water subsides, bathtub water drains) and drying occurs before the body is found. Also, drying may occur between the time the body is recovered and when it is examined by the pathologist.

Exposure to moisture causes wrinkling of the skin, which is most notable on the hands and feet ("washerwoman" skin). This wrinkling can be seen within half an hour of entering the water. This is the same wrinkling that can be observed on the hands and feet of most living people when they get out of the bathtub (or the hot tub).

The onset and course of rigor mortis is variable and will be affected by the water temperature and antemortem activity. Lividity in a submerged body is typically most prominent on the face, upper chest and the distal portions of the extremities. This livor pattern reflects the position that a human body usually assumes when submerged — i.e., back up, bent at the waist with the head and extremities dangling down. Livor may be pink, especially in bodies recovered from cold water. The rate of decomposition depends on water temperature and is generally slower than a body on land exposed to the air. Decomposition may be relatively accelerated in bacteria-laden stagnant water compared to fresh flowing water. In general, most bodies in water will not float at the surface but will be submerged. As decomposition progresses and gas is formed within the body cavities and tissues by bacterial action (putrefaction), the body will become more buoyant and will float to the surface — hence, the moniker "floater." If the water is cold enough to extensively retard bacterial proliferation, the body may never surface. Once a body is removed from water, the rate of decomposition accelerates to greater than the rate usually observed in a body exposed to the air. Even though bacterial proliferation is retarded in the water, the bacteria still disseminate and are distributed throughout the tissues. When the body is allowed to warm the bacteria (which have already disseminated) then proliferate. For this reason, it is important to examine a body as soon as possible after its removal from the water. Exposure to cold water may also hinder decomposition through the formation of adipocere.

A number of injuries may be observed on a body recovered from water. Antemortem injuries may be observed that account for death or disability. Other injuries may help reconstruct the events leading up to entering the water (e.g., sliding abrasions from skidding down the hill prior to falling off the cliff into the water; blunt force injuries inflicted during beating prior to being thrown into the water; or self-inflicted incised wounds received prior to jumping off a bridge into the water). In addition, postmortem injuries are also commonly seen on bodies recovered from the water, such as may occur from aquatic animal feeding; scraping or banging against the bottom or against objects in the water; or being struck by watercraft or their parts (e.g., propeller). Antemortem injuries may simulate postmortem ones if the hemorrhage into the tissues is leached out by the water.

Petechiae on the surface of the body can occur in drowning but are uncommon and, when present, are usually not plentiful. When petechiae do occur, they are most often found on the surface of the lungs (pleura).

The finding that perhaps is the most suggestive indication a person was alive while in the water is the presence of foam emanating from the nose and/or mouth. The foam is caused by admixing moving air with water. The foam is often white, off-white or pink (blood-tinged). The "foam cone" is often quite prominent in victims and drowning and will often reform if wiped away. Froth is also commonly found within the trachea and more distal portions of the airways. It should be recognized that the pulmonary foam/froth is not specific for drowning or breathing while submerged and may be seen in other conditions in which copious pulmonary edema is present (e.g., heroin overdose). However, in the absence of other potential causes, the presence of a foam cone is a strong indication that the victim was breathing while in the water. The absence of foam does not necessarily indicate that the person was dead when submerged.

Other nonspecific findings may also be present in the lungs. The lungs of drowning victims are often heavy because of the presence of pulmonary edema and liquid aspirated from the drowning medium. The lungs may appear hyperexpanded (they bulge from the open chest cavity during autopsy) due to the presence of water and entrapped air. The presence of water, vomitus, plant material, sand/silt in the mouth, airways, lungs or stomach is of no diagnostic significance since these materials can passively reach these locations after death.

The presence of water in the stomach or the sinuses is of no diagnostic value in determining if drowning occurred since water can reach these locations passively while the body is submerged. The presence of congestion or blood in the mastoid air cells (within the base of the skull) is also not specific for drowning.

The diagnosis of drowning is complicated by the fact that there are no specific tests to prove drowning and there are no autopsy findings that in and of themselves prove drowning. Some studies have been performed to assess the absorption and circulation of small organisms (diatoms) found within the water aspirated by the victim during drowning. At this time, these studies have not been fully validated, require special expertise and are not generally available. Other so-called drowning tests have been proposed from time to time and have been proven unreliable.

Drowning can be difficult to diagnose. However, when appropriate investigative information about the victim, circumstances and scene are coupled with the findings of the postmortem examination (including laboratory testing), a correct diagnosis can usually be made.

References

1. Graham, M.A. and Hanzlick, R., *Forensic Pathology in Criminal Cases*. Carlsbad, CA: Lexis Law Publishing, 1997.

2. Gonzales, T.A., Vance, M., Helpern, M., and Umberger, C., *Legal Medicine*. New York: Appleton-Century-Crofts, 1954.

3. DiMaio, D.J. and DiMaio, V.J.M., *Forensic Pathology*. New York: Elsevier, 1989.

4. Dix, J. and Calaluce, R., *Guide to Forensic Pathology*. Boca Raton, FL: CRC Press, 1998.

5. Modell, J.H., *The Pathophysiology and Treatment of Drowning and Near Drowning*. Springfield, IL: Charles C Thomas Publishers, 1971.

6. Spitz, W.U., "Drowning" in *Medicolegal Investigation of Death*, 3rd ed, Spitz W.U. (Ed.). Springfield, IL: Charles C Thomas Publishers, 1993.

7. Newman, A.B., "Submersion Incidents," in *Wilderness Medicine*, 3rd ed., Auerbach P.S. (Ed.). St. Louis: Mosby, 1995.

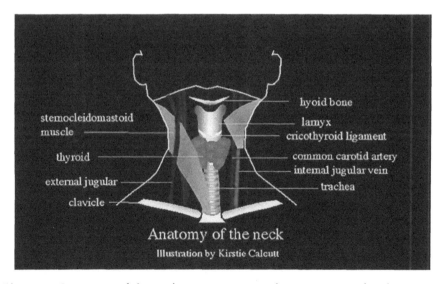

Figure 1 Structures of the neck are important to know in cases of asphyxiation. The most important structures are the larynx, trachea, hyoid bone and blood vessels.

Figure 2 There may be blood on the clothing and relaxation of the bladder and bowels in people who hang. It is also common for the decedent's feet to be touching the floor or ground.

Figure 3 A typical partially supported hanging.

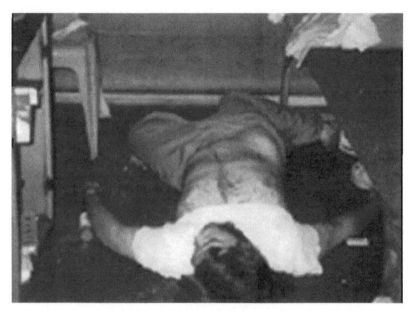

Figure 4 Most scene photographs show the people after they have already been taken down from the hanging position. See next photo.

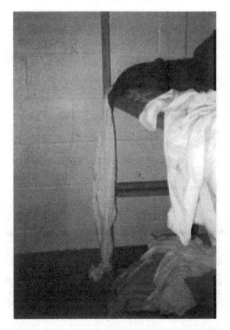

Figure 5 The man in the previous photo was not discovered hanging. When found, his buttocks were reported to be in contact with the floor.

Figure 6   This is a common presentation of a man intent upon killing himself. He kneeled down on the floor to asphyxiate himself after attaching the rope to a beam.

Figure 7   This man hanged himself from a tree in a public park. He had made other attempts in the past. The position of his arm hanging in the tree suggests he either might have changed his mind during the act or was not serious about wanting to commit the act to completion.

Figure 8 Sometimes determining manner of death is difficult. This is probably an accident; however, this cannot be stated with certainty. The boy may have been experimenting to see how it feels to choke.

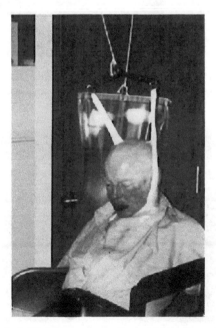

Figure 9 This retired physician used traction to ease the pain resulting from his neck problems. Autopsy revealed he had a bad heart. There was no reason to believe he committed suicide. See next photo.

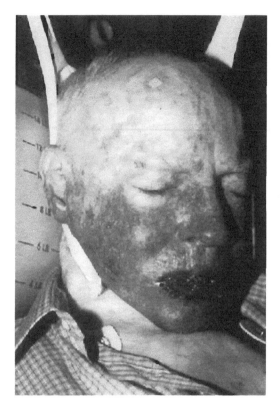

Figure 10 Lividity is on his lower face as expected. His lips and tongue have dried. There were no soft tissue hemorrhages in the neck and there were no petechiae of the eyes.

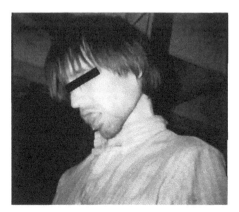

Figure 11 Typical protrusion of the tongue and drooling in hanging.

Figure 12 Typical tenting (inverted "V" pattern) of the noose.

Figure 13 This man hanged himself. His left foot is on the floor and his right is resting on the chair. See next photo.

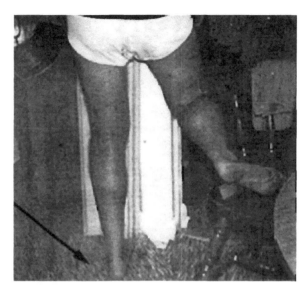

Figure 14 The feet on the floor or resting on other objects are not unusual findings. See next photo.

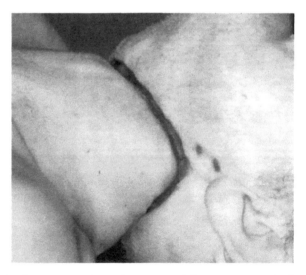

Figure 15 The ligature mark is distinct and forms an upside-down "V." The ligature mark may have a pattern of the object (in this case, a rope) or it may be very indistinct. See next photo.

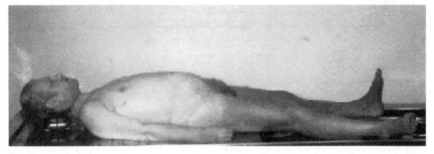

Figure 16 The livor mortis is as expected. It is concentrated in the dependent extremities. See next photo.

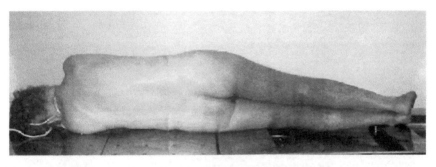

Figure 17 A posterior view also shows the dependent lividity. See next photo.

Figure 18   The left leg has many ruptured capillaries called Tardieu spots. The small blood vessels ruptured due to the pressure of gravity. Note that the right leg does not have the spots because it was resting on the chair. These spots are also seen in other parts of the body when the decedent has been dead for an extended period of time. See next photo.

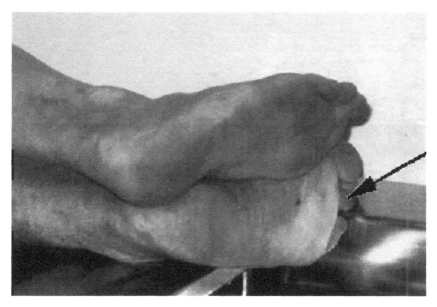

Figure 19   The bottoms of the feet also reveals which foot was resting on the chair and which was in contact with the floor. The ball of the left foot (arrow) is pale because it was resting firmly against the floor.

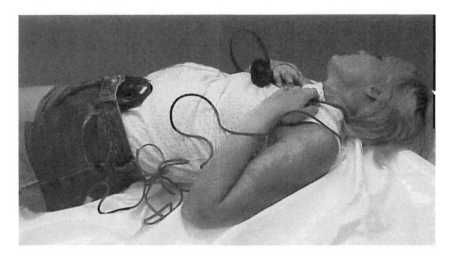

Figure 20 This woman hanged herself while listening to a tape. Notice her hands. Her fingers are between the ligature and her neck. See next photo.

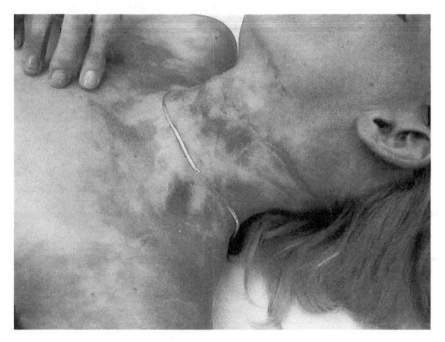

Figure 21 There are ligature marks on the sides of her neck. The marks on the front of her neck are from her fingers. The dark mark on the lower aspect of the neck is from a "hickey." See next photo.

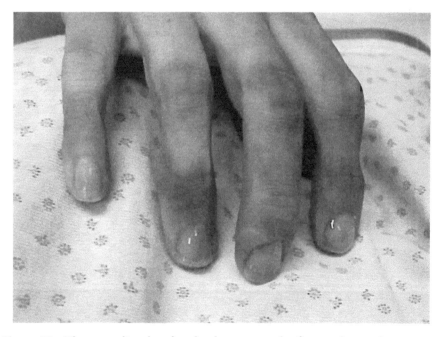

Figure 22   There are discolored and pale areas on the fingers due to the pressure of the ligature against the neck. See next photo.

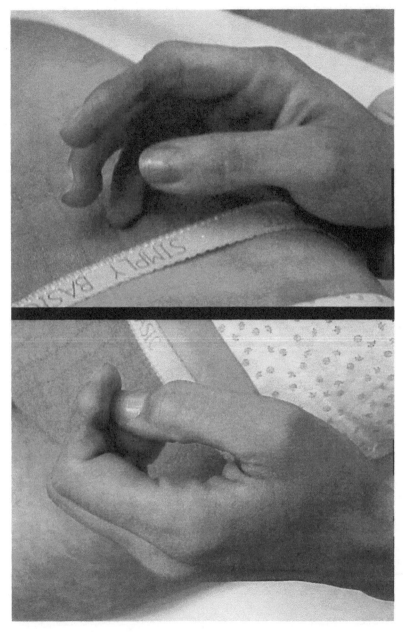

Figure 23 Note the indentations of the skin on the index and middle fingers of the right hand and index finger of the left hand.

Figure 24 This man hanged himself out in the woods. See next photo.

Figure 25 The ruling of suicide was questioned by the family because his back was against the tree and his feet were touching the ground. See next photo.

Figure 26 The scene and circumstances were consistent with a suicide. He stood on the chair to commit the act. It is not uncommon for the feet to touch the ground or some other object.

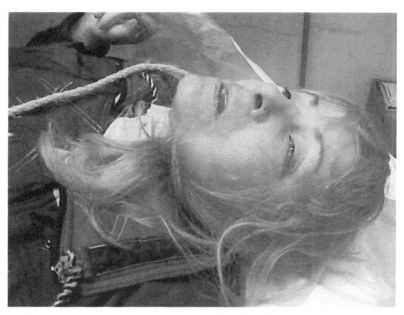

Figure 27 This woman committed suicide. Her hair is under the ligature. Perhaps the hair was used to prevent irritation from the rope or she was too intoxicated to know it was there. Her ethanol level was over 0.20 mg/dl.

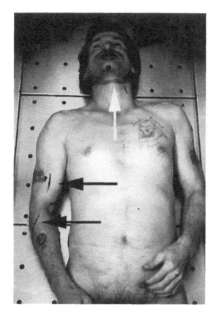

Figure 28 This prisoner attempted to commit suicide by cutting his arm (black arrows). He was unsuccessful, so he hanged himself.

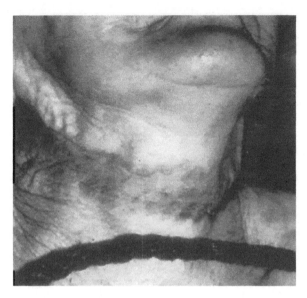

Figure 29   The rope pattern on this neck is very distinct and matches the rope. The pattern on the neck is wider than the rope because the folds of skin partially surrounded the ligature.

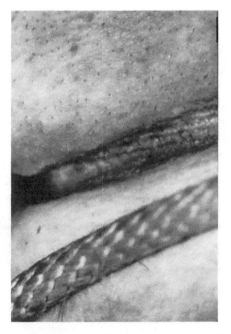

Figure 30   The depressed ligature mark has a pattern similar to the rope.

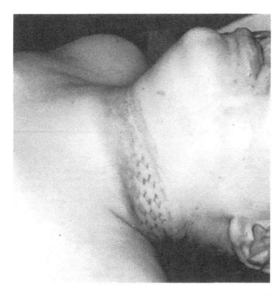

Figure 31 This ligature pattern can easily be matched to the belt that he used to hang himself.

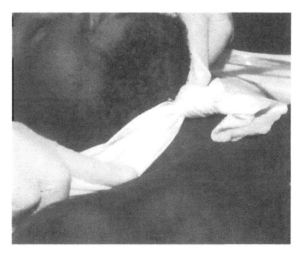

Figure 32 A knotted sheet or shirt is commonly used by prisoners. The ligature mark will not have a distinct pattern, such as one left by a rope.

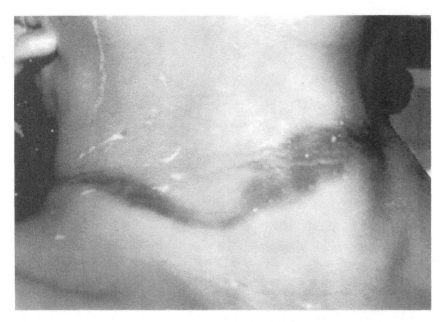

Figure 33 This is a typical nonpatterned abraded ligature mark that is commonly caused by objects such as towels, shirts, sheets, trousers, etc.

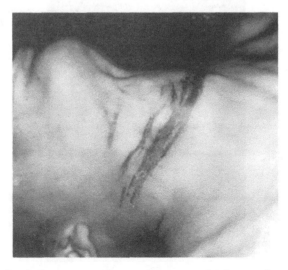

Figure 34 Multiple ligature marks may be seen in both suicides and homicides. The scene will help decide the correct manner of death.

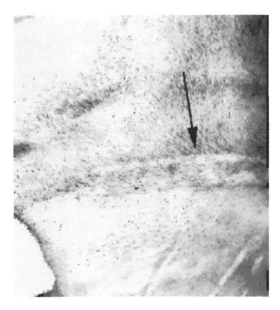

Figure 35 A shoestring wrapped twice around the neck caused these pale marks with adjacent hemorrhage.

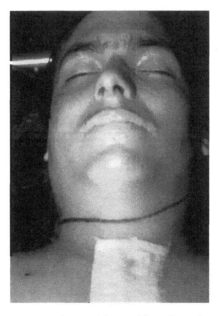

Figure 36 This military man hanged himself with a shoestring while he was stationed in Europe. He was autopsied in Europe (notice the lack of a "Y"-shaped incision. Interestingly, his neck organs had not been removed or examined.

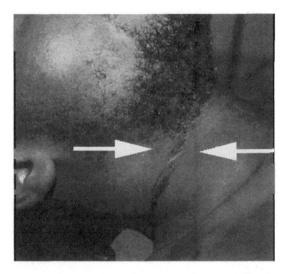

Figure 37 Ligature marks may be indistinct and more difficult to see and evaluate on dark-skinned individuals; however, this one is obvious.

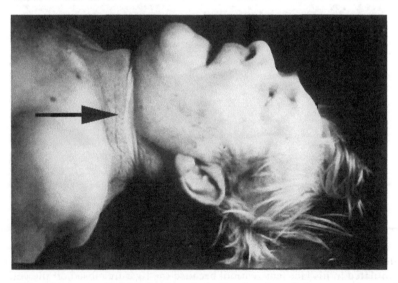

Figure 38 This man died in the hospital. On the day of the autopsy, a rubber ligature was discovered encircling his neck. The resident physician who was to perform the autopsy thought the man may have been killed. A review of the circumstances revealed the tourniquet was used to close his mouth. It had slipped down around his neck. Note the lack of congestion in his face. There were no petechiae.

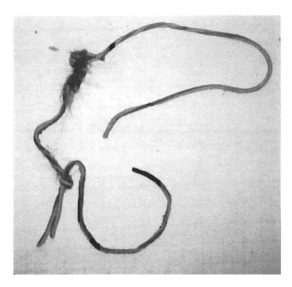

Figure 39 This ligature was removed from the decedent's neck. Note that it was cut away from the knot. The knot should be preserved.

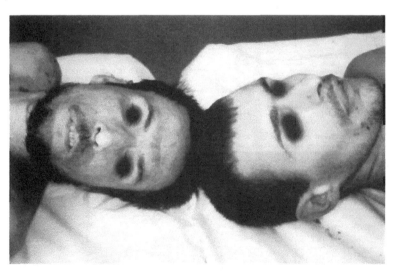

Figure 40 These two men both died by hanging. The man on the left has blood accumulated in his face (congestion) because the ligature closed off the veins and blood could still get to the head by way of the arteries. The other man's face is pale because all of the blood vessels were occluded and no blood was able to get to his head.

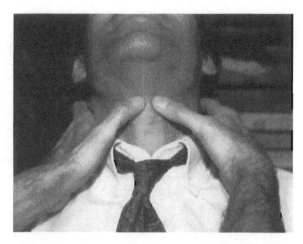

Figure 41 The hand position of the assailant on this model shows how some people are strangled manually. The thumbs may also overlap. Most people die from the pressure on the blood vessels and not from collapsing the larynx and trachea. See next photo.

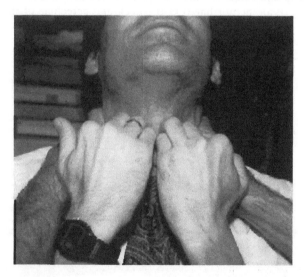

Figure 42 The victim may grasp the assailant's hands, leaving his own fingernail marks on the neck.

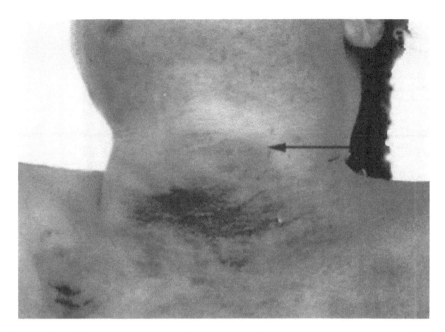

Figure 43 This man was manually strangled. There are contusions on the lower part of the neck and fingernail marks (arrow) above the contusions. There were numerous soft tissue hemorrhages in the neck and petechiae of the eyes.

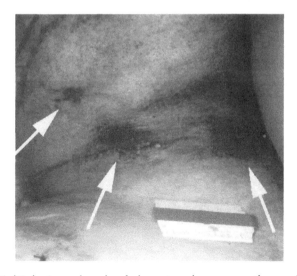

Figure 44 Multiple irregular abraded contused areas on the neck are typical marks seen in homicide strangulations.

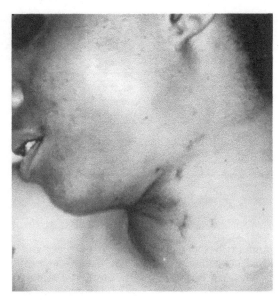

Figure 45 Some of the superficial marks on this woman's neck were caused by her own fingernails as she attempted to remove her assailant's hands as he strangled her.

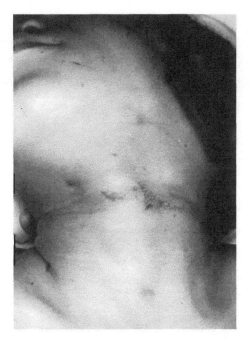

Figure 46 These indistinct marks on the neck occurred during manual strangulation.

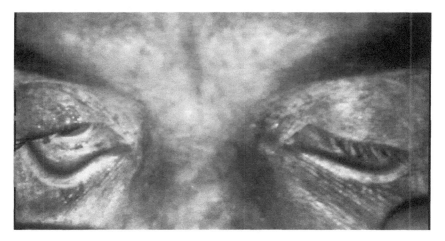

Figure 47   The pinpoint hemorrhages in this man's eyes and on the outside of his eyelids are called petechiae. Petechiae are usually present in manual strangulation, however, they can be found in other forms of asphyxiation and sudden natural death.

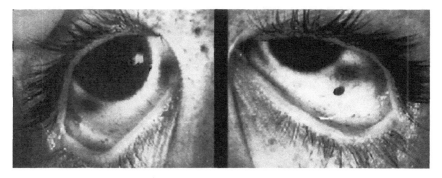

Figure 48   The petechiae in this boy's eyes occurred when he accidentally hanged himself.

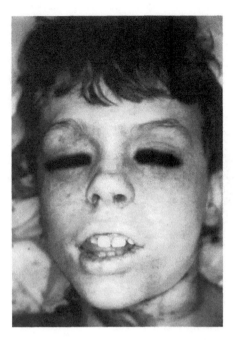

Figure 49 There are numerous petechiae around this boy's eyes as a result of an accidental strangulation.

Figure 50 The small hyoid bone (semicircular bone on the right) is located high in the neck under the chin. The pathologist looks for injury to this structure because it is commonly fractured in a manual strangulation. It is rarely damaged in hanging.

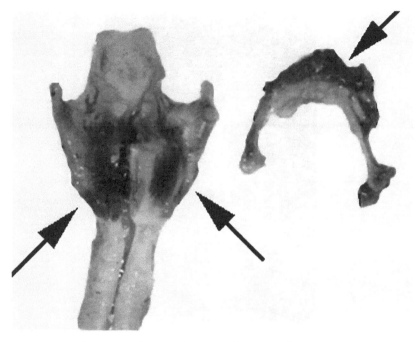

Figure 51   Another case of manual strangulation with blood behind the larynx (left) and in front of the hyoid bone (right).

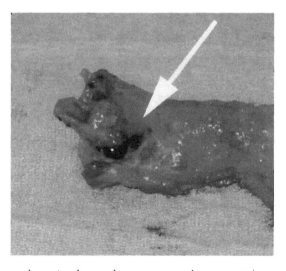

Figure 52   Hemorrhage in the neck organs may be present (arrow).

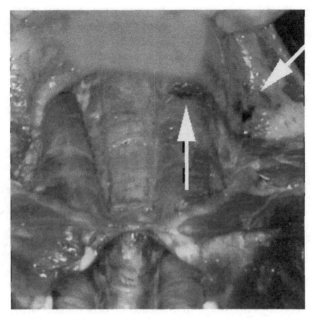

Figure 53 The soft tissue hemorrhage in homicidal strangulations may not be significant. The arrows in this case reveal small areas of hemorrhage. Petechiae of the eyes were also present.

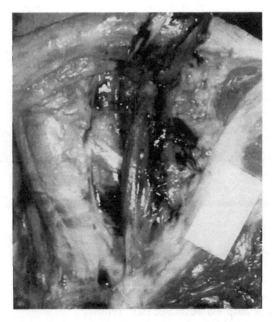

Figure 54 Impressive hemorrhage in the neck tissues, caused by manual strangulation.

Figure 55 There is hemorrhage in the base of this tongue (arrow), caused by manual strangulation.

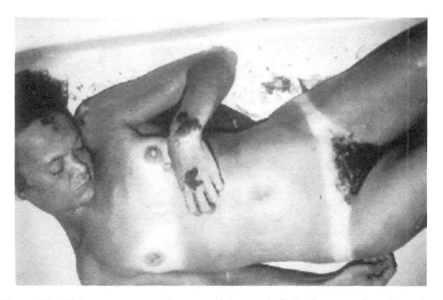

Figure 56 This woman was discovered in a tub full of water after the police went to her home with notification of her boyfriend's death. He committed suicide by inhaling auto exhaust. See next photo.

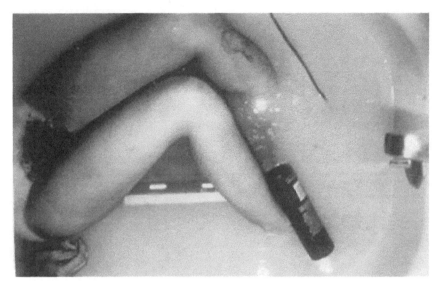

Figure 57 A radio was in the water, suggesting electrocution. See next photo.

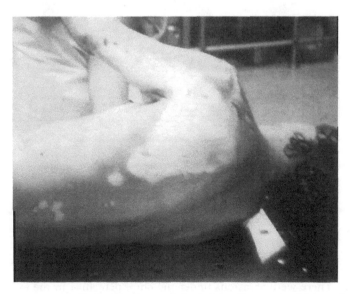

Figure 58 The water had caused significant skin slippage. See next photo.

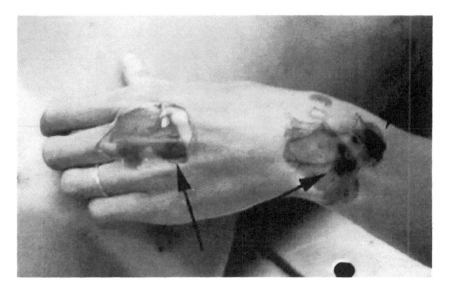

Figure 59 There were abrasions of the left hand and wrist, in addition to skin slippage. See next photo.

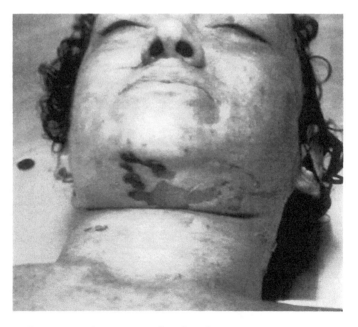

Figure 60 There were abrasions under the chin, petechiae in the eyes and soft tissue hemorrhage of the neck. She had been strangled and placed in the bathtub with a radio to make it appear that she had died of electrocution. The boyfriend strangled her and then committed suicide.

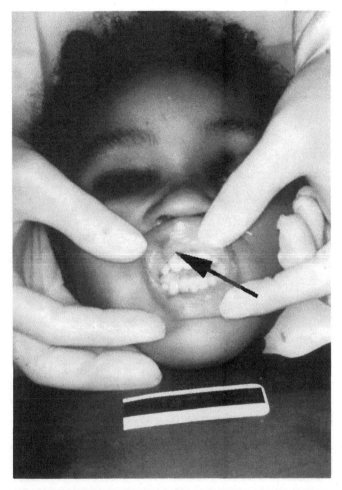

Figure 61 This child was smothered. There were very few signs of injury (arrows). Injuries such as these can also be caused by paramedics. A good history is needed to clarify this possibility.

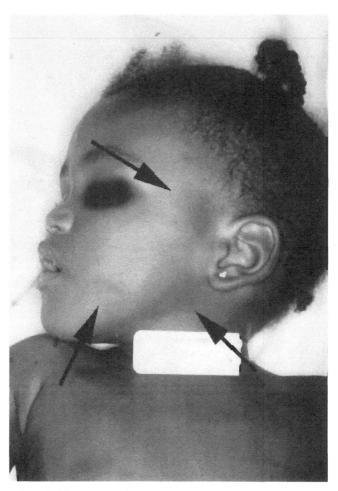

Figure 62 This child was smothered by a caretaker who placed his hand over her mouth and nose. The external signs of trauma were not very significant. There were bruises on her face (arrows) and no petechiae.

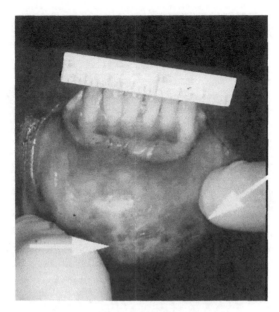

Figure 63 This child died from smothering. There are marks on the inside of her mouth (arrows) caused by pressure against her teeth.

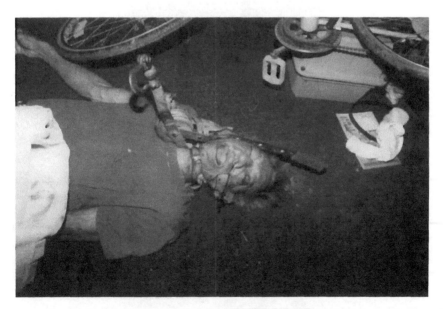

Figure 64 This man was killed by his daughter's boyfriend. The assailant said he strangled the man with a come-a-long during the fight. See next photo.

Figure 65   This is a come-a-long. It is used to move a heavy object toward another object. One end is attached to a support and the hook is attached to the object to be moved. It cannot be hooked and cranked quickly during a fight. The assailant lied about this. See next photo.

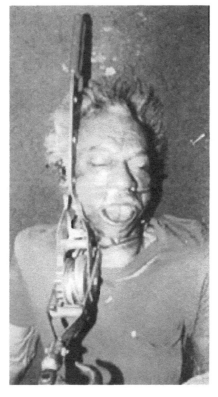

Figure 66   A closer view of the come-a-long around the decedent's neck. See next photo.

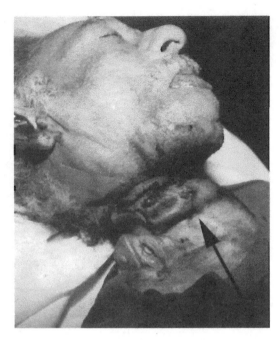

Figure 67 A closer look at the neck reveals a second abraded ligature mark (arrow) below the area where the come-a-long was tightened. This proves the man's neck was compressed prior to the assailant's use of the come-a-long.

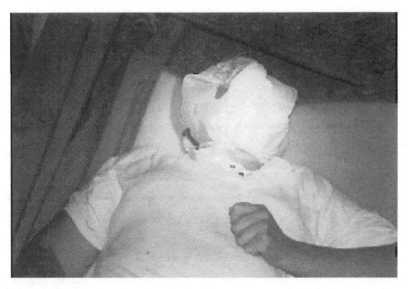

Figure 68 Asphyxiation by occluding the airway with a bag. This method of suicide is seen most commonly in the elderly.

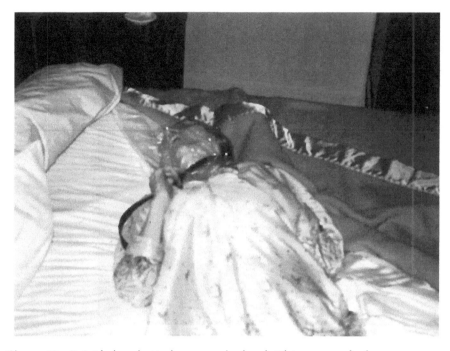

Figure 69   Suicide by plastic bag over the head. This woman had cancer.

Figure 70   In the wastebasket is the cut-off top portion of a plastic bag used in a suicide. The family had removed the bag. It was this piece that led investigators to discover that a plastic bag had been over the head.

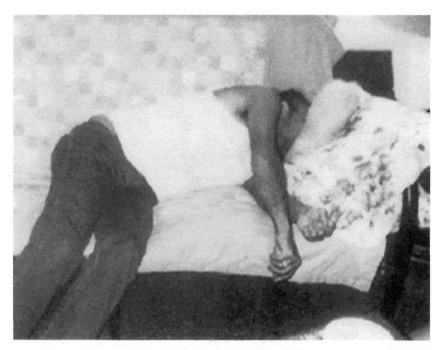

Figure 71   This man was intoxicated and fell asleep face-down into a pillow. See next photo.

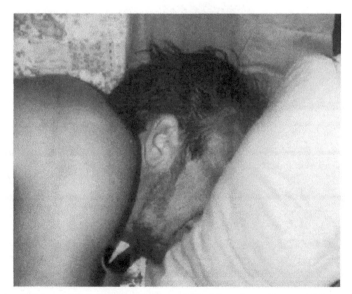

Figure 72   His nose and mouth were occluded by the pillow and he suffocated. The autopsy was unremarkable except for signs of alcoholism. The scene investigation was essential in determining the proper manner of death (accident).

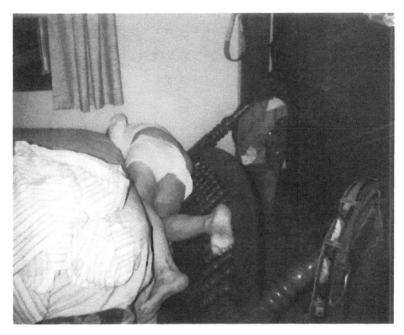

Figure 73 Another case of positional asphyxiation. This alcoholic fell out of bed and ended up in a position where he could not breathe. See next photo.

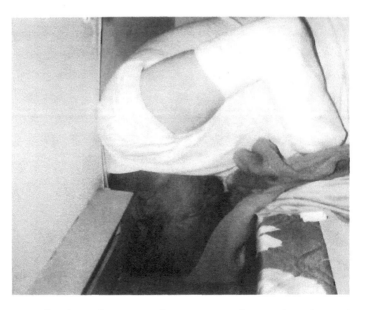

Figure 74 His head was bent enough to prevent adequate breathing. Notice the dark discoloration of his head. Death was due to blockage of the airway.

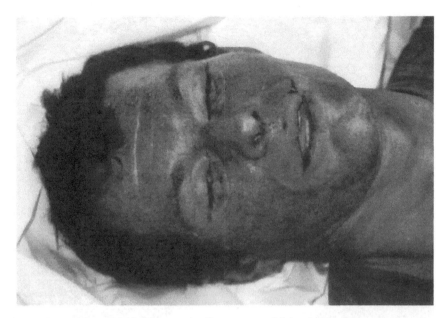

Figure 75 This man's face is markedly congested (blood-filled) because his chest was compressed by a wall that fell on him.

Figure 76 The car this man was working on fell off the concrete blocks, compressing his neck. See next photo.

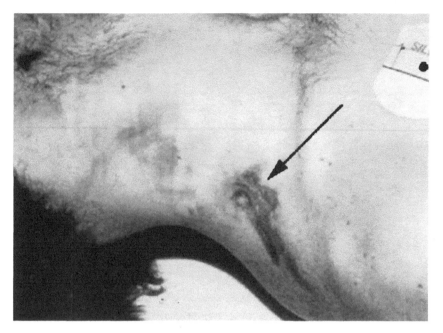

Figure 77 There were few serious injuries. The arrows point to the worst of his external injuries. See next photo.

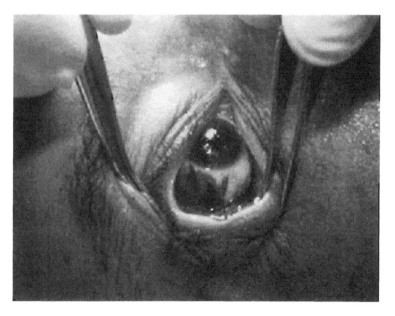

Figure 78 The pressure on his neck caused impressive hemorrhages in his eyes. The hemorrhages were not the typical petechiae seen in manual strangulation.

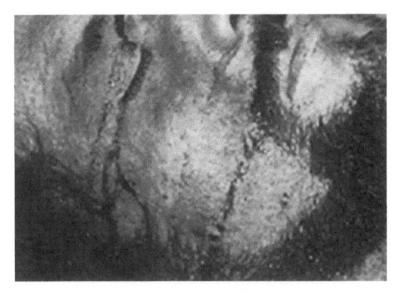

Figure 79   This man was caught under his truck after a traffic accident. His face is dark purple from blood forced up to his head under pressure. He died because he could not breathe, due to compression of his chest.

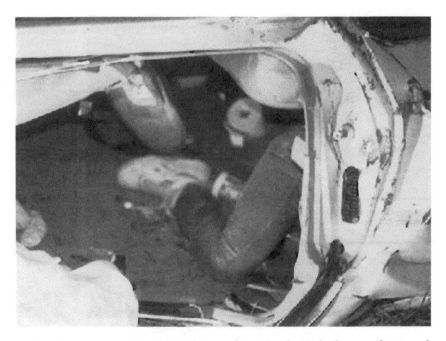

Figure 80   The body of a young man was discovered upside down in his car after the car rolled over. See next photo.

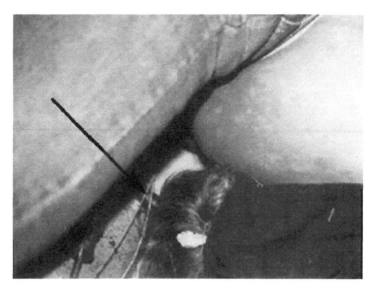

Figure 81 Note that his head is bent completely around and resting on his chest. The autopsy revealed no injuries. His neck was not broken and there were no petechiae. This is another example of postural asphyxiation.

Figure 82 This young man hopped a train. He died when metal beams shifted as the train cars were coupled. He suffocated, but there were no injuries.

Figure 83 A man (arrow) was pinned under heavy metal sheeting while he was working. There were few marks on the body and numerous petechiae of the eyes.

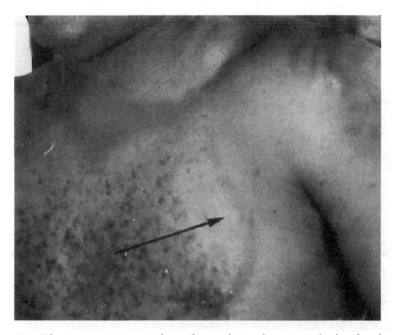

Figure 84 The arrow points to the only mark on this man's body after he was discovered compressed between the cab of his truck and the ground after an accident. He had petechiae; however, there were no internal injuries.

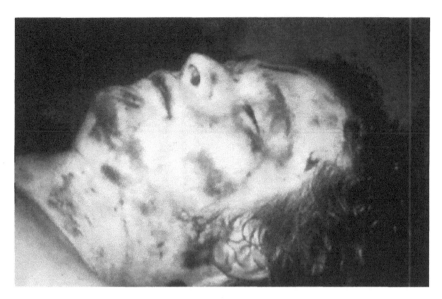

Figure 85 The abrasions on this boy's face were his only injuries. He died of suffocation after his face was compressed against another person's back during a concert where hundreds of people attempted to go through a solitary double doorway.

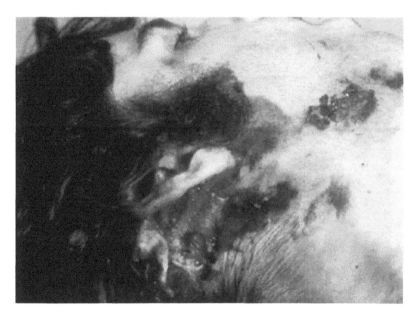

Figure 86 These injuries to the neck appear significant; however, there was little internal damage. His head was caught between the floor of an elevator and the outside door of the elevator shaft. His head was bent enough to prevent breathing.

Figure 87 This man asphyxiated as he became wedged in the window, attempting to gain access to the building. He was intoxicated.

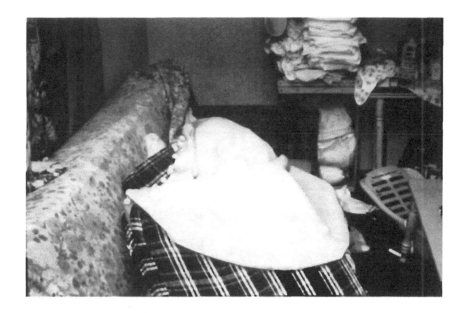

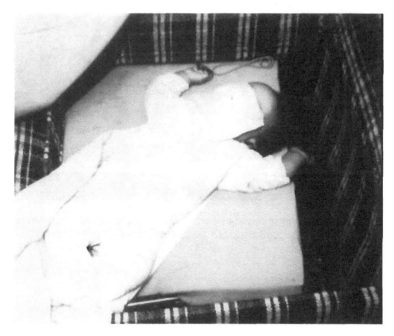

Figure 88A, 88B A woman placed her baby under the sofa cushion for protection. The mother was killed on the sofa and her weight suffocated the baby.

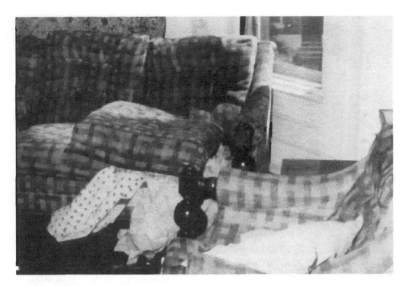

Figure 89 A baby was found under the cushion on the right. Her mother was intoxicated and fell asleep on the cushion. This is an accidental "rollover" suffocation.

Figure 90 A man was attempting to pull a log out of the woods when the log became caught and the tractor was pulled over backwards. See next photo.

Figure 91   The driver was caught under the tractor (arrow). See next photo.

Figure 92   Part of the tractor came down across the driver's neck. See next photo.

Figure 93 The driver died from a combination of traumatic crushing injuries and compression asphyxial injuries of the neck.

Figure 94 This tractor overturned as it was pulling the trailer full of rocks up the embankment. See next photo.

Figure 95 The driver was pinned under the tractor. He was asphyxiated by compression of the chest. He was not crushed.

Figure 96 This man was discovered in a landfill. He had been sleeping in a dumpster. The dumpster's contents were emptied into a trash truck and compressed.

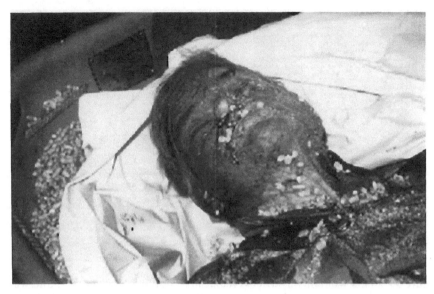

Figure 97 This man fell while shoveling corn in a silo. He died from a combination of airway obstruction and lack of oxygen in the atmosphere.

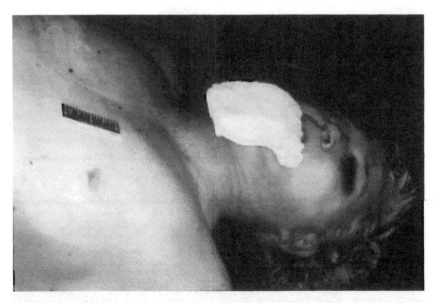

Figure 98 This woman was gagged during a robbery. The gag swelled with saliva and she suffocated.

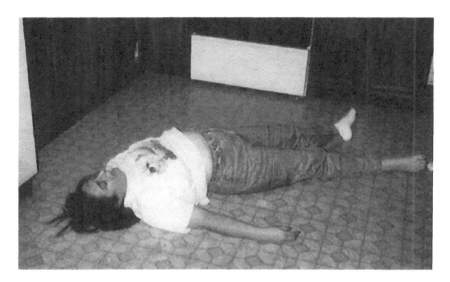

Figure 99 This woman was discovered dead at home by her mother. She was a chronic alcoholic who was known to swallow large quantities of food and then drink alcohol. She did this because she felt the food would decrease the absorption of the alcohol, thereby allowing her to remain drunk for longer periods of time. See next photo.

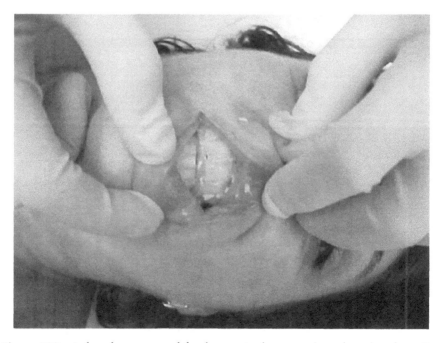

Figure 100 A few fragments of food were in her mouth and on her face. See next photo.

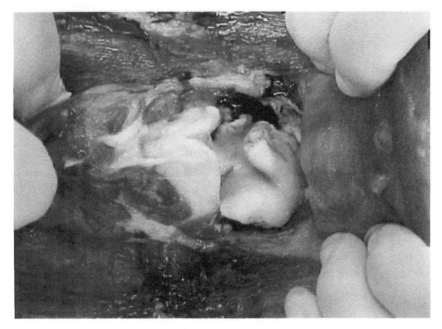

Figure 101 A bolus of turkey was lodged in her airway. See next photo.

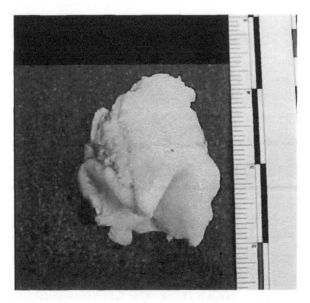

Figure 102 The wad of meat measured more than 2 by 1.5 inches.

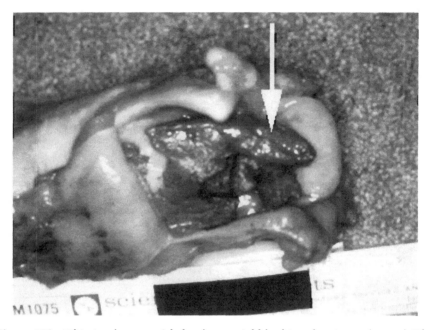

Figure 103 This is a larynx with fecal material blocking the airway (arrow). The decedent was mentally retarded and ate his feces.

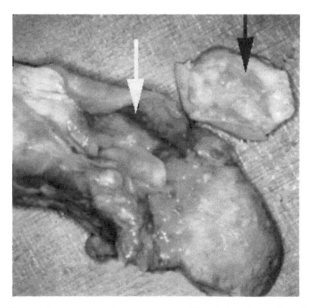

Figure 104 The white arrow points to a wad of food that lodged in the decedent's airway (black arrow). People who choke this way are usually intoxicated, mentally retarded or elderly.

Figure 105 Autoerotic asphyxiation. This young man died from compression of the neck after he lost consciousness during masturbation. There were pornographic magazines on the floor and a full-length mirror leaning against the bed. See next photo.

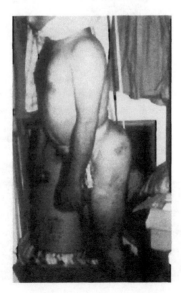

Figure 106 There was a towel around the neck to prevent abrasions and the ropes were tied in an elaborate swing-like configuration. See next photo.

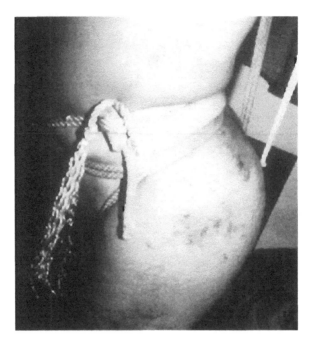

Figure 107 He had devised a slipknot to help him if he needed a quick escape. See next photo.

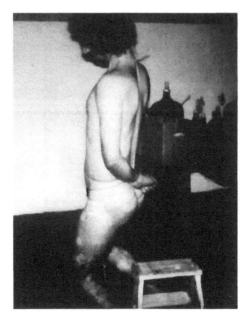

Figure 108 This naked man died of autoerotic asphyxiation. His hands were bound together with a rope that was encircling his neck and waist.

Figure 109 Another example of autoerotic asphyxiation. Notice the pad around his neck and the absence of pants. There were numerous worn areas on the beam where the rope was attached. This indicates he had done this numerous times prior to his death.

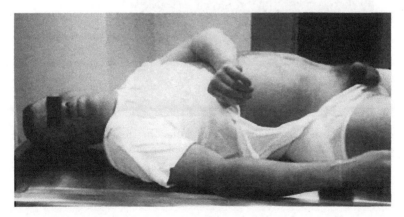

Figure 110 This soldier also died during masturbation. He had a bag over his head during the act and died from a lack of oxygen.

Figure 111 The medical examiner was called to this residence because of a suspicious death. A man was discovered "tied up" in bed. See next photo.

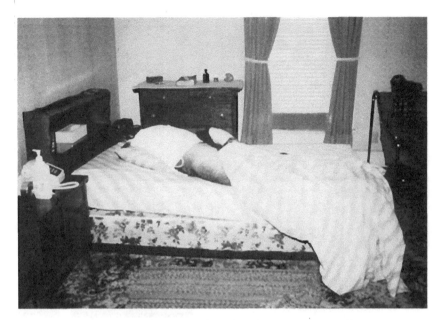

Figure 112 He was partially covered with a sheet. See next photo.

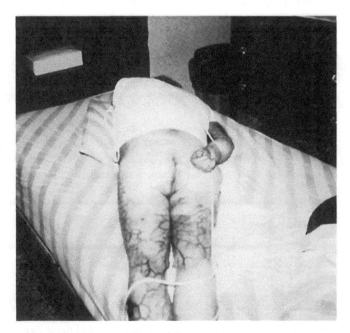

Figure 113 A rope was looped around his legs and right hand before extending up to his neck. Notice the subcutaneous marbling on his legs. He was dead at least a couple of days. The room temperature was approximately 75°F. See next photo.

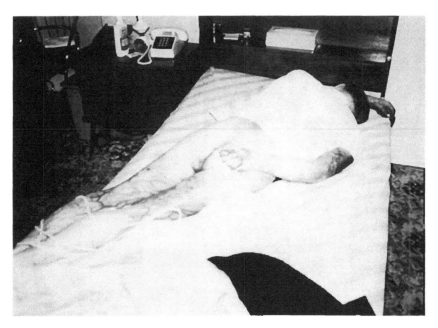

Figure 114   Another view of the position in the bed. See next photo.

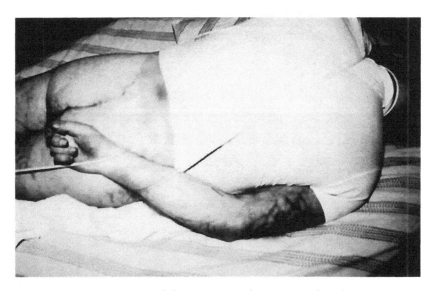

Figure 115   A close-up view of the rope around the arm and neck. See next photo.

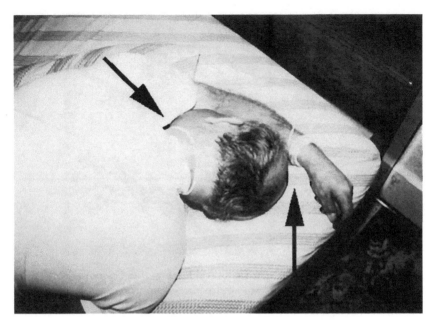

Figure 116 A closer view of the rope around the neck and left arm. See next photo.

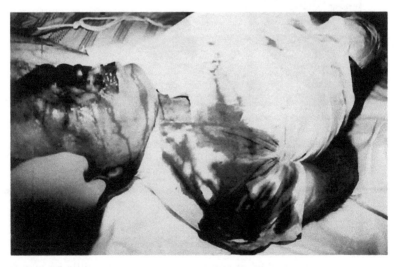

Figure 117 Blood came out his nose and mouth when he was moved. This was due to the onset of decompositional changes. See next photo.

Figure 118 Unlike other autoerotic death scenes, there was no pornographic material nearby. This magazine was in his closed briefcase.

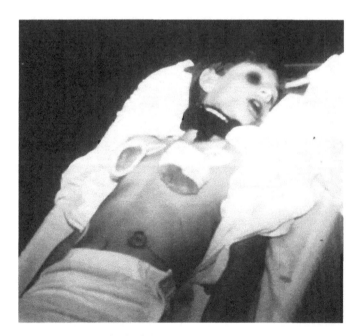

Figure 119 A young boy died of autoerotic asphyxiation while he was dressed as a woman. This is not the most common presentation of autoerotic deaths.

Figure 120 This young man was found by his family, hanging next to the bed. He was cut down prior to the arrival of investigators. There are pornographic magazines on the bed.

Figure 121 Sexual bondage, which led to asphyxiation. This was not an auto-erotic death.

Figure 122   This was a dumped body, strongly suggestive of a sexual assault and asphyxia.

Figure 123   Carbon monoxide poisoning. The man who died in this car ran a hose from the exhaust pipe into the car.

Figure 124 This is a case in which a hose was brought into the truck through the back window and secured in place with tape.

Figure 125 Most carbon monoxide asphyxiations occur in a closed environment, such as a garage. This one occurred in the open and no hoses were involved. See next photo.

Figure 126 The back seat of the car was removed and a hole was cut in the floor. See next photo.

Figure 127 The tailpipe was bent up to fit into the hole.

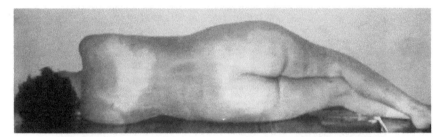

Figure 128 Carbon monoxide poisoning causes red livor mortis. Red livor mortis also occurs in cyanide poisoning and from the cold.

Figure 129 This man died from carbon monoxide poisoning. His body was burned after death. Notice the skin splits and bent elbows, wrists and knees. This pugilistc (boxer's) pose is a common artifact from the heat and does not indicate he was fighting at the time of or during death.

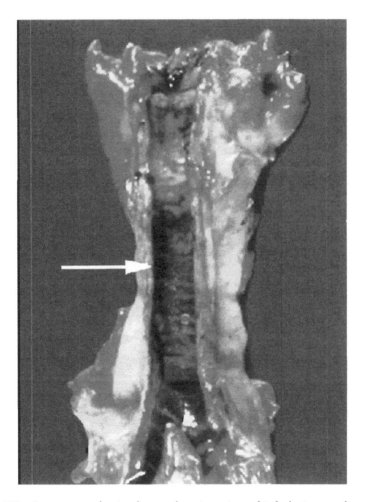

Figure 130   Soot or smoke in the trachea is a sign of inhalation at the time of
the fire. The person was alive during the fire.

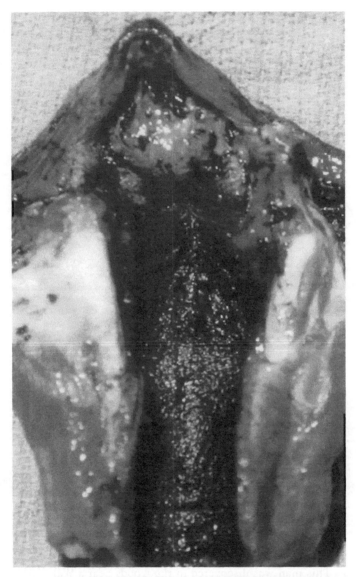

Figure 131   Another example of abundant soot in the trachea.

Figure 132 Chemical asphyxia. A faulty heater led to carbon monoxide poisoning of the entire family.

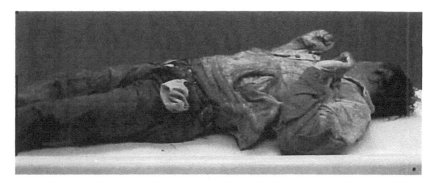

Figure 133 This man was discovered in the woods near a Wal-Mart store. Two cans of gold Rust-O-Leum and a paper bag were lying next to him. There was gold paint in the bag and one of the cans was empty. See next photo.

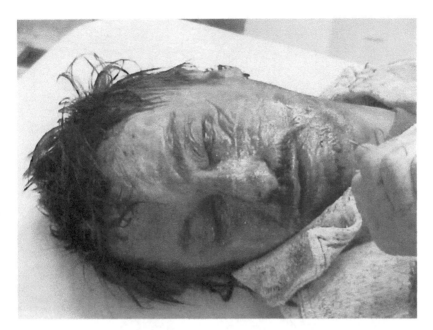

Figure 134 There was gold paint around and in his nose and mouth. He had purchased the paint the day before and was not seen that night. He had a long history of inhaling paint. See next photo.

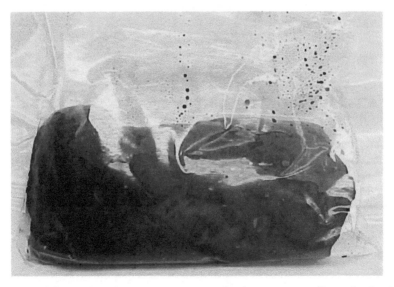

Figure 135 The material in paint is very volatile. Occasionally, volatile chemicals may be easily discovered in the blood. They may be found in lung tissue. One of the lungs in this case was collected and sealed in a bag and sent to the lab for analysis.

Figure 136 This young man was found near a railway with a plastic bag over his head. The first impression was homicide; however, his death was proven to be an accident caused by inhaling nitrous oxide from a whipped cream can.

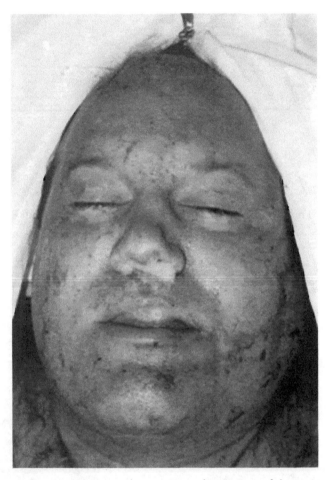

Figure 137 Drowning. Foam in the nose is a classic sign of drowning. It may be the only sign of drowning on the body. Some drowning victims have abrasions of the face, forehead, hands, feet and knees. Foam may also occur in cases of drug overdose.

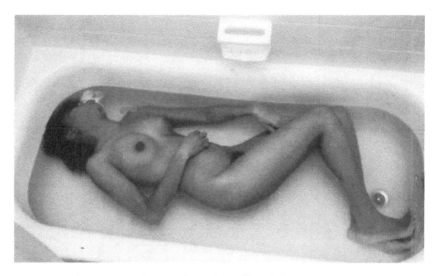

Figure 138   This woman drowned accidentally while intoxicated. An accidental death.

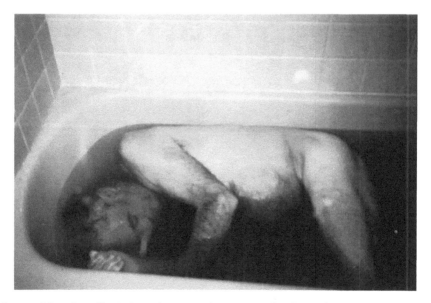

Figure 139   Not all victims discovered in water die from drowning. This man died from a rupture of the heart while taking a bath (natural death).

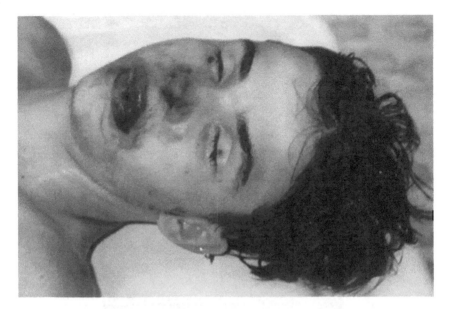

Figure 140 There are numerous abrasions, contusions, and lacerations to this boy's face and mouth. He and his uncle drowned in a shallow river during an afternoon outing with family. Law enforcement was suspicious of the circumstances because of the obvious injuries to the boy's face. See next photo.

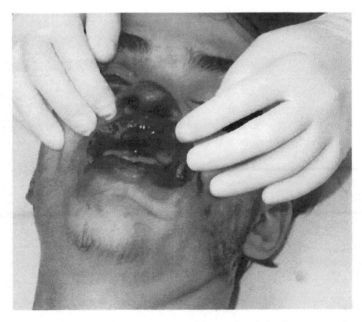

Figure 141 Injuries were also present on the inside of the boy's mouth. See next photo.

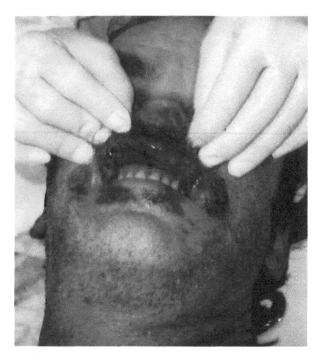

Figure 142   The boy's uncle also had similar injuries to his face and mouth. See next photo.

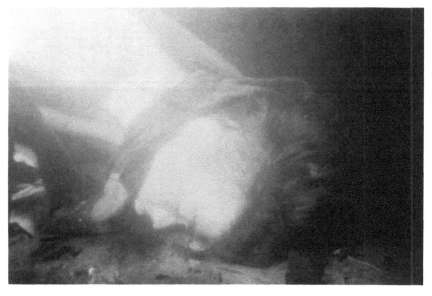

Figure 143   This is an underwater photograph showing no injuries to the boy's face as he was underwater. See next photo.

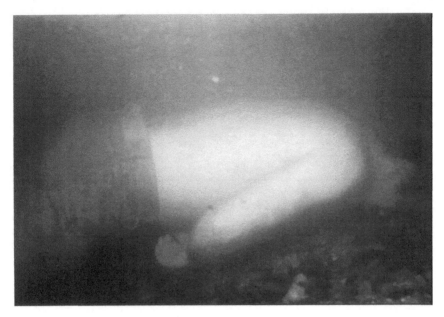

Figure 144 A photograph of the uncle underwater did not reveal any facial injuries; therefore, the injuries to both decedents occurred after death. The injuries were caused by the face impacting and scraping against the bottom of the river.

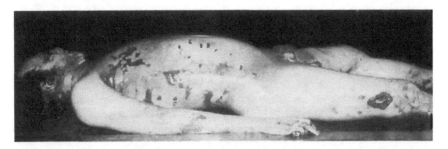

Figure 145 This man drowned and the body was not discovered for 3 weeks in the wintertime. The injuries to the body occurred after death.

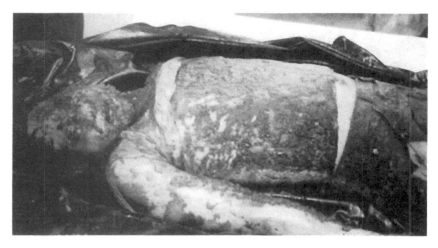

Figure 146 Abundant moss covered most of this young man's body after only 3 weeks in a pond. See next photo.

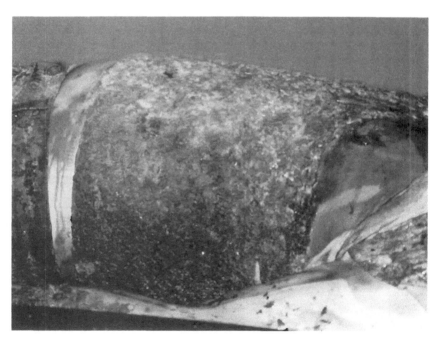

Figure 147 The moss was especially thick on the trunk. It had to be scraped away to look for injuries. See next photo.

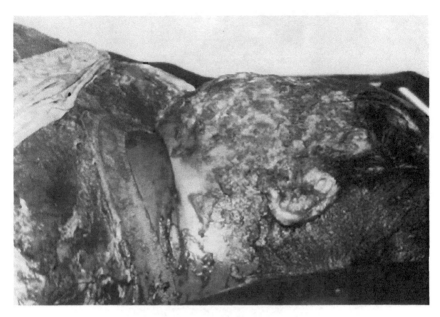

Figure 148   There was also plenty of moss on the face. See next photo.

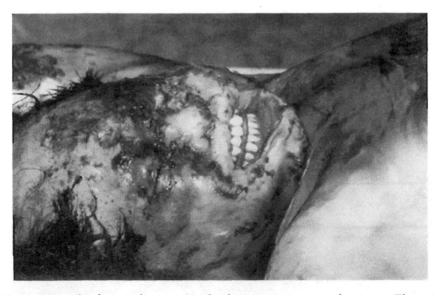

Figure 149   The face and upper trunk after scraping away the moss. There is good exposure of the mouth and teeth. Injuries are difficult to evaluate in these types of cases when decompositional changes occur.

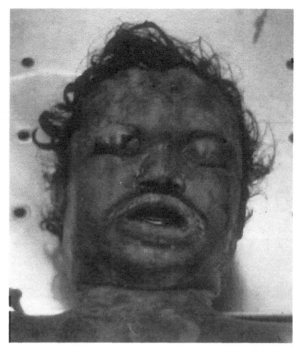

Figure 150 This young white man drowned in a river and was not found for 4 to 5 days after death in the early fall. There were no signs of drowning. See next photo.

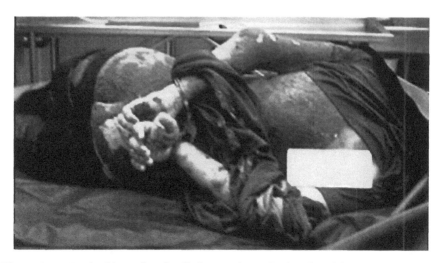

Figure 151 He had been handcuffed, struck on the head and forced into a river.

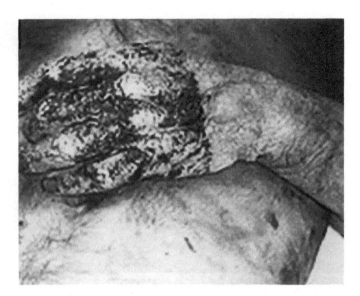

Figure 152 Wrinkling of the skin from drowning. Notice the rest of the body does not have this change. The feet had skin slippage like the hands.

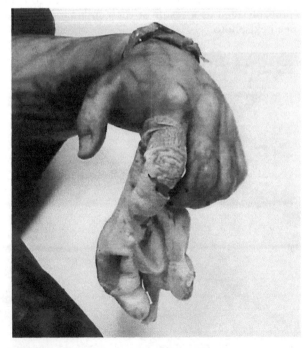

Figure 153 Marked wrinkling and skin slippage. The slipped skin can easily be used for fingerprinting if needed.

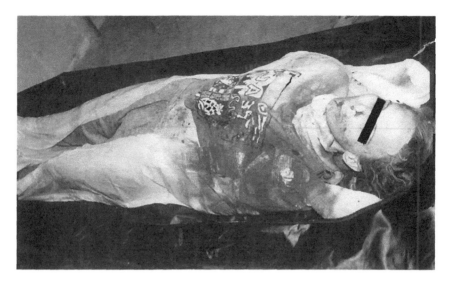

Figure 154 A mother and her two children were killed by two teenagers. Their bodies were discovered in a pond near their home. The mother was bound after being raped, and her throat was cut. There was abundant clotted blood under her shirt, proving she lost a considerable amount of blood prior to being thrown in the water. She probably died as a result of the combination of exsanguination and drowning. See next photo.

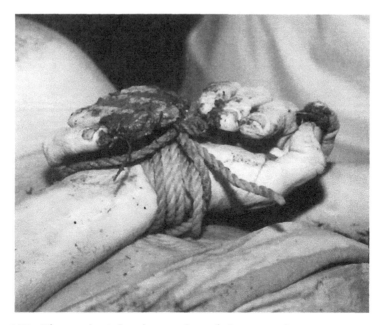

Figure 155 The mother's hands were bound. See next photo.

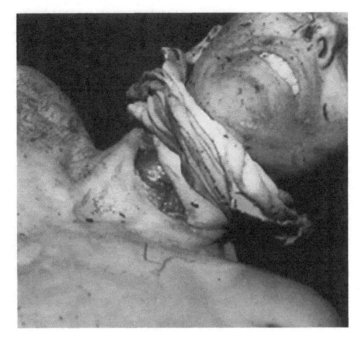

Figure 156 Incised wounds of the mother's neck. The gag over her mouth had slipped off by the time of the autopsy. See next photo.

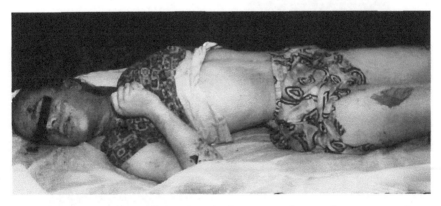

Figure 157 The 14-year-old daughter had no incised wounds. See next photo.

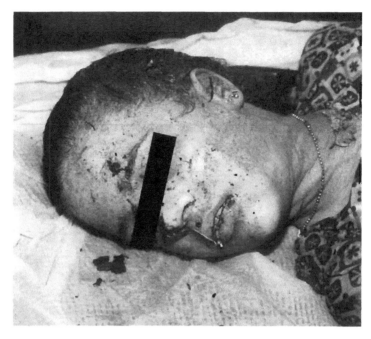

Figure 158   She had a chain around her neck which left superficial bead markings. See next photo.

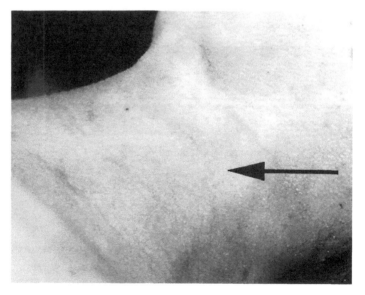

Figure 159   The faint bead markings from the necklace (arrow) were the only signs of trauma to her neck. See next photo.

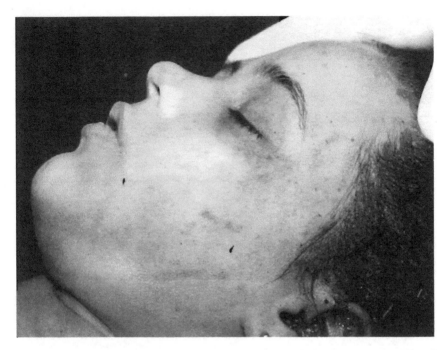

Figure 160 She had multiple petechiae of the face, especially around and in the eyes. These extensive petechiae are more indicative of a forceful compression than a straightforward drowning. One of the assailants later admitted to forcing the girl's face down into the water and mud after she attempted to escape.

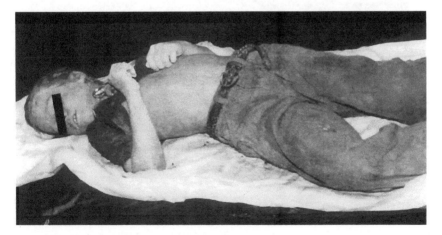

Figure 161 The 11-year-old son's neck had also been cut. There was no blood on his clothing. He died from drowning. See next photo.

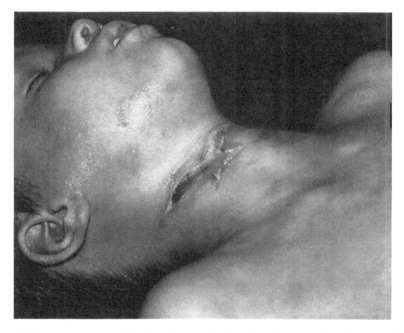

Figure 162   A close-up of the boy's neck, indicating the superficial nature of the cuts. His neck was cut just before he was thrown into the water.

T - #0602 - 101024 - C0 - 229/152/7 - PB - 9780849323690 - Gloss Lamination